NATIONAL TRUST STUDIES 1979

National Trust Studies 1979

Sotheby Parke Bernet

© The National Trust 1978

First published 1978 for
Sotheby Parke Bernet Publications by
Philip Wilson Publishers Ltd,
Russell Chambers, Covent Garden, London WC2

Edition for the USA available from
Sotheby Parke Bernet Publications,
c/o Biblio Distribution Center,
81 Adams Drive, Totowa, New Jersey 07512

ISBN: 0 85667 051 0

Editor
Gervase Jackson-Stops

Designed by Paul Sharp
Printed in England by Robert Stockwell Ltd, London, SE1 1YP

Foreword

LORD GIBSON, *Chairman of the National Trust*

One of the unique features of the National Trust is the breadth of the activities and interests that it encompasses. Its work brings together people of entirely different backgrounds and skills whether young or old, expert or amateur. *The National Trust Yearbook* was first launched in 1975 to give more publicity to the serious research work which is constantly going on behind the scenes into historical and scientific aspects of our properties. It was felt then that this would be of interest not only to other specialists, but to a large section of the general public who shared the Trust's aims and ideals and wished to know more about its work. After the success of the three initial volumes in the series, its scope has now been enlarged still further, thanks to the support of Sotheby Parke Bernet & Co. who have given a generous grant towards its costs, and who have undertaken the production of the book in conjunction with Philip Wilson Publishers.

A new title, *National Trust Studies*, has been chosen both because it describes this collection of essays accurately, and because it avoids confusion with the Annual Report sent out each year to members. At the same time it indicates a change in the appearance of the book. Uniformity with the earlier Yearbooks has been preserved in the page size, but the dust jacket and layout of this volume have been redesigned, there are many more pages and, for the first time, colour plates have been included. All this has been achieved with only a very modest increase in cost.

The subjects covered by this year's articles range from wild birds to rare books, and from firearms to neo-classical farmyards. These are some of the many different fields in which the Trust constantly benefits from the researches of independent scholars as well as its own staff. The articles touch upon the architecture and contents of newly acquired houses, such as Soane's work at Wimpole, and portraits by Mengs at Dunham Massey and Mount Stewart; they describe new discoveries at properties of long standing – amongst them a seventeenth-century English bronze at Ickworth and a pair of statues commissioned by Louis XIV at Cliveden – and they reveal little known aspects of other houses, like the literary associations of Stourhead and the musical traditions of Knole. John Cornforth's assessment of the contribution made by the late John Fowler also provides an important chapter in the Trust's own history.

With something for every taste, I am certain that members of the Trust, and many other people, will find *National Trust Studies* a fascinating and rewarding book, and I look forward to many further volumes in the series.

Contents

Foreword
Lord Gibson, Chairman of the National Trust   5

The British Portraits of Anton Raphael Mengs
Francis Russell   9

Edward Goudge: 'The Beste Master in England'
Geoffrey Beard   21

John Soane, Philip Yorke and their Quest for Primitive Architecture
Pierre de la Ruffinière du Prey   28

John Fowler and the National Trust
John Cornforth   39

Firearms at Felbrigg
D. H. L. Back   51

'Mr Warren' and the Wrought Iron Gates at Clandon and Powis
Edward Saunders   60

Birds and Man on the County Antrim Coast
Philip S. Watson   67

High Victorian Horticulture: the Garden at Waddesdon
John Sales   77

Companions of Diana at Cliveden
Terence Hodgkinson   91

Thomas Hardy and Stourhead
Roger Alma   99

Rebuilding Stourhead 1902–1906
Dudley Dodd   113

Hubert le Sueur's Portraits of King Charles I in Bronze,
  at Stourhead, Ickworth and elsewhere
Charles Avery   128

The Lucys of Charlecote and their Library
Henry Summerson   149

Music at Knole
Wyn K. Ford   161

Notes on Contributors   181

Acknowledgments   183

Robert 1ᵗ M. of Londonderry

8

The British Portraits of Anton Raphael Mengs

FRANCIS RUSSELL

'Mengs has done but few pictures for England except copies.' This rather sweeping statement of the anonymous translator of the 1796 London edition of d'Azara's *The Works of Anthony Raphael Mengs* is true only in the limited sense that the painter's work for English patrons represented but a small fraction of his total output. The writer's list of Mengs's English commissions runs to a mere ten items and of these only one is a portrait,[1] a statistical abberation that casts a revealing light on his comprehension of the artist's role, for the latter in fact painted self-portraits for Lord Cowper and Sir William Hamilton and a series of portraits of English travellers, second in interest only to the great sequence of such pictures by Batoni. The National Trust has recently received two notable portraits by Mengs, one at Dunham Massey (Fig 4), the other at Mount Stewart (Fig 1), and it is thus appropriate that these, preserved now in their proper homes, should also be considered in the context of Mengs's portraiture.

Mengs and Batoni were regarded by many theorists of the time as the greatest of living painters. Their fame was founded on what they achieved in Rome but, unlike his rival who was permanently based there, Mengs lived in the city only intermittently. Born in 1728 he first was taken to Rome by his father in 1740, returning to Dresden in 1744. By 1746 he had won the favour of Augustus III of Saxony and could return, with the security of a royal pension, to Rome, where he stayed until the autumn of 1749. After some three years in Dresden he was able once again to travel, reaching Rome in May 1752. A sojourn of 1759 in Naples apart, he remained in the city until the summer of 1761 when he was called to Spain by King Charles III. Not until 1769 did he return to Italy, journeying by way of Genoa and Florence to Rome where he spent much of 1771 and the following year. Late in 1772 he paid a second visit to Naples and then set out by way of Rome for Florence where he arrived late in 1773. From there he departed once again for Madrid in the ensuing year, staying until 1776 when he finally returned to Rome where he was to die in 1779. This peripatetic existence had a direct bearing on Mengs's availability for Grand Tour commissions and his migrations therefore establish the framework within which his British portraits should be reviewed.

Mengs's first English sitter, painted at Dresden, was Sir Charles Hanbury Williams, the diplomat and friend of Horace Walpole. Several of his later patrons must, like Walpole, have seen the prime version of the portrait at Lord Essex's, and Sir Charles's example was followed by other English travellers after Mengs returned to Rome in 1752. The restrained *Richard Wilson*, now at Cardiff, is of that year and in the ensuing winter or early spring, Mengs worked for Anthony Langley Swymmer, a rich Member of Parliament who seems to have been drawn, however fleetingly, into the tortuous web of the Elibank plot. Swymmer's portrait has disappeared but that of his beautiful wife Arabella is at Dalmeny. Richly dressed and set against an appropriate backcloth, she offers a foretaste of the formal portraits Mengs would paint for the court at Madrid.

The urn and landscape of the Dalmeny picture show how promptly Mengs responded to the challenge of Batoni in a field which the latter had so spectacularly made his own in the previous half dozen years. Both artists were fully conscious of their rivalry and it seems possible that at least one influential member of the English artistic colony at Rome, Thomas Jenkins, consciously sought to build up Mengs's practice. A letter of 1760 from Thomas Robinson shows how carefully he reviewed the work of the two

1 *Robert Stewart* by Mengs, 1758–59 (National Trust, Mount Stewart)

painters before determining to sit to Mengs and four richer Englishmen, the Duke of Richmond, William Fermor, Sir Brook Bridges and Lord Brudenell had previously evaded making such a decision by sitting to both.

Mengs's Grand Tour portraits were at no time so numerous as those of Batoni but several of the more discriminating connoisseurs who visited Rome in the years before 1761 sat to him. Thus, in 1755, he painted the young Duke of Richmond, whose portrait in Van Dyck costume at Goodwood makes an obvious contrast with the less formal character of Batoni's somewhat earlier pictures at Goodwood and Melbury, Robert Wood of Palmyra fame and Adam's companion the Hon Charles Hope. William Fermor, the Catholic owner of Tusmore in Oxfordshire, who befriended Skelton the water-colourist during his visit to Rome, sat for an unusually restrained portrait in 1757–58 (Fig 2). The latter year was unusually productive: Mengs painted whole-length portraits of Sir Brook Bridges, Lord Brudenell and, probably, the latter's cousin the Duke of Manchester, besides half-lengths of Lord Garlies and Lord Brudenell, both in Van Dyck costume, of Brudenell's tutor Henry Lyte and Thomas Conolly of Castletown.

These portraits are very varied in character. The *Duke of Manchester* at Kimbolton with its columns and strategically placed map of Italy contrasts somewhat awkwardly with so assured a work as Batoni's *Lord Northampton* of the same year in the Fitzwilliam.

3 *Lord Brudenell* by Mengs, 1758 (Boughton House, the Duke of Buccleuch and Queensberry)

The *Thomas Conolly*, of which two autograph versions exist, is more direct in presentation and memorable for the splendid richness of its blue drapery, while the *Lord Garlies* is strangely reminiscent of Ramsey. The fine and perceptive portrait of Henry Lyte was evidently painted with considerable sympathy, but Mengs was clearly very conscious of the competition he faced with his pictures of Bridges and Lord Brudenell.

Of Mengs's whole lengths, that of Bridges is both the most convincing and the most compelling comment on the convention of the Grand Tour. Bridges stands on a terrace on the Janiculum, with a tree to one side and a distant view of St Peter's to which he points at the other. He is resplendently dressed in a red velvet coat, lined with ermine, velvet breeches of the same colour and a waistcoat of oyster silk brilliantly embroidered in crimson. Mengs does not seek to match the intimacy of Batoni's picture. Indeed he seems deliberately to trump his rival's hand, indulgent no doubt of the taste of a young man who appears to have bought no pictures in Italy, the two portraits apart, and is known to have escaped from his fellow countrymen in the company of an Italian mistress.

Mengs's whole-length portrait of Brudenell (Fig 3) and the half-length by Batoni still hang in adjacent rooms at Boughton. Both are of 1758 and despite their different scale they offer a fascinating insight of the rivalry of the two artists. The Batoni is a picture of unusual distinction, beautiful in colour and defined with a precision so

4 *Lord Grey* by Mengs,
1760 (National Trust,
Dunham Massey)

extraordinary that the score Lord Brudenell holds can not merely be identified as that of
a sonata by Corelli but can actually be played. Mengs is altogether more austere. Brudenell
sits before a table, dressed in a sombre red coat, the patterned fur lining of which is
realised with an almost obsessive care. With him are the dog and bust that were to
become the quintessential extras of Grand Tour portraiture and a narrow glimpse of
landscape behind. The presentation is predictable enough but Mengs's solution was
clearly the climax of a rigorous intellectual progression in which his sitter may well have
shared. It is in this connection significant that Brudenell sat twice to Mengs and
ironical that Batoni's portrait should establish that they had an important taste in
common. For d'Azara states that on the morning Mengs commenced his *Annunciation*
for Aranjuez, now in the Palacio Real at Madrid, he and Christopher Hewetson, the
sculptor, found that the painter 'was practising a sonata of Corelli's, because he wished
to finish this painting after the style of Music of that great Composer'.[2] The Boughton
picture does not directly allude to music but the carefully balanced structure of its

design is indeed directly paralleled in the work of Corelli and his contemporaries. More than any other portrait of the kind, its evinces the cerebral character that Winckelmann sensed in Mengs's art.

The painter's classicism is less forcefully stated in the smaller portrait of Brudenell at Beaulieu and none of his later Grand Tour commissions is indeed conceived in so elevated a spirit as the Boughton picture. Their mood is restrained and their presentation more relaxed, as if to suggest that the artist had tired of the obvious conventions of Grand Tour portraiture.

Of the National Trust's new portraits, the more accomplished is that of Robert Stewart, subsequently the 1st Marquess of Londonderry, at Mount Stewart (Fig 3). Unfortunately, the final digit of the date accompanying Mengs's signature cannot be read, but it seems likely that the portrait is of 1758 or the following year.[3] The likeness is as benignly observed as that of Lord Garlies and the arrangement of the hands and splendid flowing draperies give the picture a monumental character which is conspicuously lacking in the portrait Batoni was to paint of the sitter's brother Alexander, which is also at Mount Stewart.[4]

The canvas of Lord Grey at Dunham Massey (Fig 4) is less imaginative. He stands holding a book in a rather wooden posture and his dress is somewhat mechanically described. Lord Grey's travelling companion was his neighbour Sir Henry Mainwaring of Peover, who sat not to Mengs but to Batoni. A miniature of the two friends was painted by Mengs's sister at the cost of 60 zechins in 1760 and she supplied a further miniature of Sir Henry for 12 zechins a year later. Both purchases were made through Thomas Jenkins and a series of letters to Sir Henry from both Jenkins and his friend and rival antiquary Daniel Crespin, which have recently come to light at Dunham Massey, casts a fascinating light both on the services they had tendered at Rome and the range of the interests both Mainwaring and Grey had evinced there. Crespin kept Sir Henry closely informed of the comings and goings of the English colony in Rome and confirms that like his friend he had known Mengs. On 3 June 1761 he reports:

> Mengs has quite finished the Ceiling at Villa Albani, it is much admired: He is to copy for some Lady in England, but I know not who, the Bacchus and Ariadne in the Capitol, And as this is Supposed to be either Sketch or Copy only of Guido its imagined his picture will far exceed it.

Even after Mengs's migration to Madrid, news of his movements reached Rome. On 27 November, Crespin was able to retail this:

> Mengs has set out happily in Spain, his reception there most gracious, a Present of three thousand Crowns from the Dowager Queen, in return for a Magdalen he had carried over with him. I fancy his sister will be likely to be called to Madrid in the Spring; a Miniature Picture of hers, he presented to the King, was much admired.

Mainwaring and Grey had of course left Rome over a year before but Jenkins continued to execute commissions for them and Crespin's correspondence, with its accounts of later visitors, of Mengs and Batoni and English artists in Rome, clearly constituted a sort of post-Grand Tour service. Mengs's place in this is thus a telling mark of his reputation at the time of his departure for Spain.

The letters to Mainwaring give some flavour of the relationship Mengs could have with a discriminating and serious patron and a pastel of the young William Burton

5 *William Burton, later Conyngham* by Mengs, probably about 1760 (Private Collection)

(Fig 5), who was later to be so crucial a figure in Irish architectural circles, offers further evidence of this. Framed in the eighteenth-century as pendant to a version of Rosalba's portrait of Lord Boyne, it may well have been commissioned as a pair to this picture, which would explain both the unusual medium (no other pastel of a British sitter by Mengs is known) and the measurements. But if the painter had to adhere to such specifications he was allowed to achieve his own interpretation. More than any of Mengs's other Grand Tour commissions the portrait has the air of his many self-portraits and pictures of his friends, partly because of the simplified, indeed almost neo-classical, draperies he uses. Executed with the precision of Liotard and with its admirably preserved colour, the subtle reddish grey of the cloak set off by the blue of Conyngham's coat and his white shirt, the pastel must rank as one of Mengs's most satisfying portraits.

Both Grey and Mainwaring knew Thomas Robinson who determined to sit to Mengs in the summer of 1760. They may also have met a yet more remarkable connoisseur, Edward Bouverie, whose portrait at Longford must have been painted not long before Mengs's departure. With its Roman altar, this picture may be regarded as the last of Mengs's Grand Tour portraits. For his later pictures of British sitters were to be commissioned and considered in a rather different spirit. Thus the *Louis de Visme* now at

Christ Church, Oxford, was painted at Madrid and the *Earl Cowper*, now in the Corsini Collection, at Florence, where the sitter resided for so many years.

When Mengs left for Spain his mantle fell on his erstwhile pupil and brother-in-law Anton Maron, whose practice was to become in a sense no more than an extension of his own. Maron's portraits are of uneven interest, but that of Robert Fitzgerald, later 17th Knight of Kerry (Fig 6), who was in Rome in 1765, is a wholly successful venture in the manner of Mengs. With Maron's portrait of Sir Horace Mann in the Cornwallis collection it may be viewed as an appropriate epilogue to the sequence of Mengs's English portraits.[6]

6 *Robert Fitzgerald* by Maron, 1765 (Private Collection)

Catalogue of portraits

Hon Edward Bouverie (1738–1810)
Collection: Longford Castle, the Earl of Radnor

Bouverie was a notable connoisseur and acquired an extensive collection of drawings, partly it seems in Italy. According to a letter of 9 October 1762 from Sir Horace Mann to Walpole he was then about to return to England from Florence: the portrait therefore probably dates from shortly before Mengs's departure for Spain in the summer of 1761.

Literature: *Catalogue of the Pictures in the Collection of the Earl of Radnor*, II (1909), no. xli.

Sir Brook Bridges, 3rd Bart of Goodnestone (1733–91)
about 225 by 162.5 cm
Private collection

Bridges is recorded at Padua in June 1757 and had reached Turin on his homeward journey by November 1760 (information from Brinsley Ford). The half-length portrait by Batoni is dated 1758 and Mengs's unusually ambitious picture is presumably of the same time (Mengs's authorship was first noted by Anthony Clark).

John, Lord Brudenell, later Marquess of Monthermer (1735–70)
240 by 168.7 cm
Collection: Boughton House, the Duke of Buccleuch and Queensberry

Lord Brudenell sat to both Mengs and Batoni in March 1758 (*Il Settecento a Roma* (1959), p 154). A reduced copy of this portrait is at Bowhill.

Literature: John Fleming, 'Lord Brudenell and his Bear Leader', *English Miscellany*, IX (Rome, 1959).

John, Lord Brudenell
95 by 71.2 cm
Collection: Beaulieu, the Lord Montagu of Beaulieu

Like the preceding portrait this is of 1758.

William Burton, later Conyngham (1733?–1796)
pastel, 65 by 48.7 cm
Private collection

This splendid and unusually well preserved pastel seems to have been painted as pendant to Rosalba's portrait of Lord Boyne, probably for the 1st Earl of Leitrim, who sat to Batoni in about 1754. Burton was also painted by Dance.

Thomas Conolly, of Castletown (1738?–1803)
signed and dated 1758, 128 by 92.5 cm
Collection: Castletown, Hon Desmond Guinness

Painted no doubt early in 1758, before Conolly's return and marriage to Lady Louisa Lennox, sister of the Duke of Richmond (*qv*). Recorded in the possession of Conolly's mother by Walpole ('Mr Conolly, to the knees, with a bas relief, at Lady Anne Conolly's, in Grosvenor-square'), the picture was presumably installed in its present position when the Gallery at Castletown was decorated by Riley in the 1770s.

A signed autograph replica of this portrait which descended through the Clancarty family was sold in 1974 (Christie's, 3 November 1974, lot 13).

Literature: Horace Walpole, *Anecdotes of Painting in England*, V (1937), (edited by F. W. Hilles and Philip B. Daghbian), p 52.

George, 3rd Earl Cowper
Collection: Florence, Palazzo Corsini

Dated 1773 by Voss, this portrait was certainly executed during the artist's visit to Florence in 1773–74. A related canvas has recently been acquired for the Mellon Collection. The self-portrait painted for Lord Cowper, formerly at Panshanger and now at Liverpool, is of 1774 and there is evidence of other commissions at this time. To judge from a photograph, however, the attribution to Mengs of a small full-length portrait of Lord Cowper sold from Panshanger in 1955 (Christie's, 16 October 1955, lot 93) is doubtful.

William Fermor of Tusmore (1737–1806)
61.2 by 45 cm
Collection: P. and D. Colnaghi & Co

Walpole records that Fermor sat to both Mengs and Batoni ('Mr Farmer, a Roman Catholic, son of lady Brown, has his own portrait both by Mencks and Pompeio'). The Mengs is dated 1757 on the stretcher and both pictures must have been painted before 28 June 1758 when Fermor is stated to have been 'on his way home' in a letter of

Jonathan Skelton, the watercolourist. (Brinsley Ford, 'The letters of Jonathan Skelton', *Walpole Society*, XXXVI (1960) p 47). The Mengs, the identity of which is established by inscriptions on the stretcher, only resurfaced in February 1978 (Anon. sale, King & Chasemore, Pulborough, 7 February 1978, where purchased by Colnaghi). Iconographic analysis suggests that a signed portrait of 1758 in the Kress collection at Houston may be the missing Batoni (F. R. Shapley, *Paintings from the Samuel H. Kress Collection, Italian Schools XVI–XVIII Century* (1973), p 120, fig 238).

Literature: Walpole, p 52.

Father Gahagan (d1774)
61.2 by 46.2 cm
Untraced, formerly at Wardour Castle

This portrait was evidently commenced by Mengs prior to his departure for Spain in 1761. Only the head was finished. This was acquired by Father Thorpe who arranged in 1771 for Maron to finish the drapery. Finally the picture was dispatched to Wardour in 1774 (Information from Brinsley Ford).

John, Viscount Garlies, later 7th Earl of Galloway (1736–1806)
signed and dated 1758, 100 by 75 cm
Collection: Cumloden, the Earl of Galloway

A letter of 5 April 1758 from John Parker establishes that Garlies had already reached Rome and he is recorded at Turin in the latter part of the year (Information from Brinsley Ford). He commissioned a copy of the version of Titian's *Venus and Adonis* then in Palazzo Colonna and now in the National Gallery, no. 34, from Mengs's pupil James Nevay (*Idem*). He may also have purchased a *Saint John Preaching* which was attributed to Mengs in 1825 (Earl of Galloway sale, Christie's, 12 February 1825, lot 80).

George Harry, Lord Grey, later 5th Earl of Stamford (1737–1819)
inscribed and dated 1768 by a later hand, 95 by 72.5 cm
Collection: Dunham Massey, the National Trust

Despite the inscription this portrait must have been painted in 1760 when Grey and his companion and neighbour Sir Henry Mainwaring were both in Rome. They arrived at Rome from Naples 9 February and were in Florence in July (Information from Brinsley Ford), subsequently travelling to Venice and Pola.

Hon Charles Hope (1710–91)
Untraced

Hope, with whom Robert Adam travelled until they quarrelled in September 1755, reached Rome on 24 February 1755. Mengs's portrait of him is referred to in a letter of 18 September from Colin Morrison to his patron Lord Deskford in which it is further stated that Hope has 'also purchased the Seasons painted in Crayons for my Lord Hopetoun, extremely fine of the kind' (Seafield MSS. C. & G. D. 248/954/5. I am indebted to Brinsley Ford for this reference).

Henry Lyte (1727–91)
88.7 by 72.5 cm
Collection: London, Brinsley Ford

Painted in 1758 when Lyte was in Rome as governor to Lord Brudenell (*qv*)

Literature: *Il Settecento a Roma* (1959), no. 380, pl 70.

George, 4th Duke of Manchester (1737–88)
Collection: Kimbolton Castle

Walpole, who also records the present portrait, states that Batoni's whole length of the Duke in 'Roman habit' was 'drawn about the year 1760'. Both were probably of 1758–59.

Literature: Walpole, pp 20 and 52; A. Oswald, 'Kimbolton Castle', *Country Life*, 26 December 1968, illustrated p 1598.

Mr Mann
Untraced

George Willison, who was in Rome in 1760–67 and studied under Mengs, sold a group of pictures at Christie's, 4 March 1773. Lot 19 was listed as by 'Minx' and described as 'A portrait, Mr Mann, fine'. This was purchased by Reed or Rud for 11s. Mengs was recommended to Horace Mann by Sir Charles Hanbury Williams in 1752.

Charles, 3rd Duke of Richmond (1735–1806)
128.7 by 92.5 cm
Collection: Goodwood, the Earl of March

The Duke, who was also painted by Batoni, graduated at Leyden in 1753. He was at Rome 26 March 1755 but had returned to England by the end of the year.

Thomas Robinson, later 2nd Lord Grantham (1738–86)
Untraced

Robinson, who evidently knew Lord Grey (*qv*), arrived in Rome in 1759. He announced his decision to sit to Mengs rather than Batoni in a letter of 9 August 1760 to his father in which the merits of the two artists are compared.

Literature: G. Beard, *Leeds Art Calendar* (1960), no. 44.

Robert Stewart, later 1st Marquis of Londonderry (1739–1821)
signed and dated 1758(?), 100 by 72.5 cm
Collection: Mount Stewart, the National Trust

Anthony Langley Swymmer, MP (?1724–60)
Untraced

Swymmer, who had inherited a Jamaica fortune, set out for Rome from London accompanied by his wife Arabella (*qv*) in September 1752. He commissioned a picture of Flora from Mengs and had left Rome by 21 April 1753 (Information from Brinsley Ford).

Arabella Swymmer, later Lady Vincent (?–1785)
Collection: Dalmeny, the Earl of Rosebery

One of Mengs's most successful female portraits this was painted at the same time as the lost pendant.

Louis de Visme (1720–76)
123.7 by 83 cm
Collection: Christ Church, Oxford

De Visme was at Madrid in 1762–67. In a letter of 20 December 1763 to Horace Mann, he refers to Mengs's health and the portrait may date from this time (PRO State Papers Foreign 105/315. I am indebted to Brinsley Ford for this reference).

Literature: Mrs Lane Poole, *Catalogue of Oxford Portraits*, III, (1925), p 70, pl 3.

Daniel Webb, of Maidstown Castle (1719–98)
Untraced

Webb seems to have been in Rome in 1754-55: by 24 June 1755 he was at Bologna on his return journey (Information from Brinsley Ford). d'Azara records that he took advantage of Mengs's friendship to copy his manuscript treatises on painting and plagiarise these. Webb's *An Inquiry into the Beauties of Painting* was published in 1760 and first exposed by Wincklemann. The lost portrait is recorded by both Jansen and Prange and is perhaps to be identified with the *Portrait of a Gentleman in the Character of an Architect*, now at Prague, which was formerly in the Kilmorey collection (Earl of Kilmorey sale, Sotheby's, 3 December 1924, lot 15).

Sir Charles Hanbury Williams (1708–59)
Untraced

The portrait was executed at Dresden and is first mentioned in a letter of July 1752 from Lord Essex, the sitter's son-in-law, in whose possession both it and a miniature 'in watercolours') are recorded by Walpole. An autograph version, formerly in the collection of Stanislas Poniatowski and now at Warsaw, is published by Honisch (D. Honisch, *Anton Raphael Mengs* (1965), pl 8).

Literature: Walpole, p 52.

Richard Wilson (1714–82)
82.5 by 73.7 cm
Collection: Cardiff, National Museum of Wales

Painted at Rome in 1752.

Literature: D. Cooper, 'The Iconography of Richard Wilson', *Burlington Magazine*, 90 (1948), pp 109–110, fig 13.

Robert Wood (1711–71)
73.7 by 62.5 cm
Collection: Mertoun, the Duke of Sutherland

Wood reached Rome by 17 January 1755 and in the following months is known to have kept company with Robert Adam and Charles Hope (*qv*). The portrait was painted for the Duke of Bridgewater.

Notes

1 The list is appended to the translator's preface and the picture is recorded as a 'portrait of the late Bishop of Salisbury', presumably John Hume, who was translated to the see of Salisbury in 1766 and died in 1782.

2 J. N. d'Azara, *The Works of Anthony Raphael Mengs* (1796), I, p 34.

3 I am grateful to Miss Daphne Cunningham for checking this inscription.

4 This unsigned and apparently unrecorded picture was brought to my notice by Gervase Jackson-Stops.

5 I am indebted to Gervase Jackson-Stops for enabling me to study this correspondence.

6 This note could not have been prepared without the generous help of Lady Aldington, the Dowager Duchess of Buccleuch, Miss Clements, Adrian Fitzgerald, Lady Fitzwalter, John Hammerbeck, Sir David and Lady Scott, Rafael Valls and Clovis Whitfield and no mere acknowledgement can acquit my debt to Brinsley Ford.

1　Belton, Lincolnshire. The ceiling of the Staircase, *c* 1688. Plastered by Goudge for Sir John Brownlow

Edward Goudge:
'The Beste Master in England'

GEOFFREY BEARD

When Margaret Jourdain wrote her *Decorative Plasterwork of the Late Renaissance* in 1926 she made brief mention of the talented plasterer Edward Goudge. He had lamented on 25 March 1702 that

> for want of money occasioned by the War, and by the use of ceiling painting, the employment which hath been my chiefest pretence hath been always dwindling away, till now its just come to nothing. . . .[1]

It is the purpose of this article to chronicle Goudge's career and to note his work at Petworth House, West Sussex, and his possible work at another National Trust property, Dunster Castle, Somerset.

Goudge seems to have had an early connection with the architect Nicholas Hawksmoor. Vertue records[2] that Goudge did 'some frettwork ceilings' at Justice Mellust's[3] house in Yorkshire, and that he there met Hawksmoor, who was 'Clerk to Justice Mellust'. It seems possible that Goudge then introduced him to London circles. But as for Goudge himself his fame does not seem to have been due to any firm connection with the Office of Works, or with Sir Christopher Wren. As far as can be established his name does not appear in the records of the Worshipful Company of Plaisterers[4] and his origins and apprenticeship details are unknown. He was principally employed by the architect Captain William Winde (d 1722) from the early 1680s.

Winde was born at an unknown date before 1647 at Bergen-op-Zoom in Holland of English parents. He came to England at the Restoration in 1660. He had already made the army his main career, and apart from a brief period as a gentleman usher in the service of Elizabeth, Queen of Bohemia, daughter of James I, he managed with some adroitness to be both officer and architect. On 12 June 1688 he wrote to his cousin, Lady Mary Bridgeman, whose Warwickshire house at Castle Bromwich he was remodelling, to recommend Goudge.

> This bearer is Mr Edward Gouge & is the Person I recomended to yr Ladp att Bromingen. he dide the frett seallings att Combe and I will assure yr Ladyp no man in Ingland has a better Tallent in ye way [of plastering] than hime selfe hee has bine imployed by mee this 6 a 7 yeares, is an excelent drauffteman and mackes all his desines himeself. . . .

Within a few months he was further commending Goudge to Lady Mary. Writing on 8 February 1689–90 he indicated that

> Mr Goudge will undoughtedly have a goode deall of worke for hee is now looked on as ye beste master in England in his profession as his worke att Combe, Hampsted & Sir John Brownlowes will Evidence.

Winde's letters[5] are invaluable for recording in a chatty way what the craftsmen he was involved with were doing. Admittedly this was usually on commissions he was engaged in, such as his work for Lord Craven, but on 27 April 1691 Goudge himself writes to the Bridgemans to apologise for his tardiness about the commission – one of his reasons was that his man David Lance was 'at the Duke of Sumersetts at Dettworth [Petworth] in Sussex'. Lance became Master Plasterer to the Office of Works in 1708, but in these 'apprenticeship years' he assisted Goudge to plaster the barrel-vaulted ceiling of the

2 Petworth House, the Chapel, 1685–92, from an old photograph (before restoration). The barrel-vaulted plasterwork ceiling is by Edward Goudge

Chapel (Fig 2) and worked also in the Marble Hall. Some of their work elsewhere in the house may well have perished in the fire of 1714, or been destroyed in the mid eighteenth-century alterations carried out by the 2nd Earl of Egremont.

The unpublished correspondence between Winde and his cousin Lady Mary Bridgeman gives a good idea of Goudge's movements. He was employed by the 2nd Earl of Clarendon at Swallowfield, 1689–91, a house designed by William Talman. Some of the work was delayed by Goudge's illness, and it was also noted by Winde that the plasterer needed to go to view the fall of building-work in 1689 at Hampton Court.

As well as being a successful plasterer Goudge supplemented his income by acting as a clerk-of-works for building works. In 1689 he was employed in London by the Derbyshire landowner, Thomas Coke of Melbourne. Coke, who later became Vice-Chamberlain to Queen Anne and George I, married Lady Mary Stanhope in 1698. Whilst he was away after his marriage his house in St James's Place was enlarged by adding the adjoining house.

Goudge was put in charge of the work but did not care for the design he was to work on. He therefore prepared one of his own. The humdrum nature of his duties included many menial tasks. His letters at Melbourne[6] show how he took care that the household necessities and the cooking equipment were all ready for Coke's household to use. He also had to be tactful and resourceful, for Coke's neighbours, particularly Lord Godolphin, were angry at the rebuilding, and Godolphin threatened Goudge's workmen with a pistol if their arms as much as strayed over his land whilst they were wielding hammers on the boundary wall.

The Melbourne letters are as unhelpful as most when Goudge wrote to Coke on 17 August 1698 that he had a job at Rochester 'that will imploy me 3 or 4 days in a weeke for about 3 weekes'. It may well be that he was working at Rochester Guildhall or assisting Winde in work at Eastwell for Lord Winchelsea, but there can be no certainty of this in view of his abilities as a builder.

We have mentioned Winde's letter in which as an indication of Goudge's standing he instances the plasterer's work at Combe, Hampsted Marshall and Belton House. Lord

3　Edward Goudge, signed drawing for the Dining Room ceiling, Hampsted Marshall, Berkshire, 1686 (Bodleian Library, Oxford)

Craven's letter-book[7] in the Bodleian Library records faithfully the negotiations he entered into with Winde for the rebuilding of Combe Abbey, Warwickshire from 1678 to 1684. It also reveals Winde's surprising inattention to the task in hand. On 6 March 1681/2 Lord Craven wrote to Winde inviting him to Combe to see the foundations of the house laid. However this necessary visit does not seem to have been undertaken by Winde. By 10 July 1682 he has also still not sent the correct plans to Lord Craven. The workmen were at a standstill for want of direction and Lord Craven indicated that he would need to discharge them if positive direction was not forthcoming. Combe is a good example of the erection of a house which only proceeded by the owner's active intervention in what might properly have been regarded as his architect's business. Fortunately the somewhat one-sided interchange of letters shows that Lord Craven was diligent in pressing on with the work. By 5 February 1682/3 Winde was advised that sufficient timber for the stairs had been sawed and stored. The letters also indicate that Edward Pearce, a carver of great ability, and Goudge were at work. Winde and Pearce had recommended Goudge to Lord Craven and he was also Winde's choice when he was called to work at another Craven property, Hampsted Marshall.

The system which Winde's master, Sir Bathazar Gerbier, had advocated in his *A Brief Discourse concerning . . . Magnificent Building* (1662), of the master workman keeping his men short of pay to prevent them absconding to other work, does not seem to have been followed with diligence by Winde. He placed great reliance on the skill and acumen of his master craftsmen and inspected all designs. The signed drawing[8] (Fig 3) by Goudge for the Dining Room ceiling at Hampsted Marshall is endorsed across the centre: 'June 22th: 1686. This Drauft for the Dineing Roome att Hampstead Marshall marked A allowed of by me Will.Winde'. The letter we have cited provides confirmation of Winde's known attendance at the Craven properties, but the reference to Goudge at 'Sir John Brownlowes' is valuable in suggesting him as the author of the fine plasterwork at Belton House, Lincolnshire (Figs 1, 4) which Sir John Brownlow was having decorated, 1686–88. It also hints to us that the master-mason in charge of the work there, William Stanton, a statuary of some note, was possibly supervised by Winde.

The Bodleian drawing by Winde, and the extant work by Goudge at Belton and
Castle Bromwich led Mr Howard Colvin to suggest that some drawings (Figs 5,6) in the
collection of the Royal Institute of British Architects were by Goudge.[9] Comparing the
illustrations of two of them with the Hampsted drawing (Fig 3) shows that the attribution is the best solution so far advanced. Unfortunately the ceilings they represent
have not been identified – the demolition of Hampsted after a fire in 1718, and the
dispersal of the Combe interiors by sale in the early 1920s removed some of the likely
sources. They bear a stylistic resemblance however to the fine ceilings at a National
Trust property in Somerset, Dunster Castle (Figs 7-9), which was rebuilt from 1680
onwards.

It has been shown that the owner of Dunster in the 1680s was Colonel Francis
Luttrell.[10] Both he and Winde fought at the Battle of Sedgemoor in June 1685, and
through their respective army careers may have known one another in earlier years. The
Dining Room ceiling at Dunster is incised with the date '1681' in Roman numerals. Its
authorship must remain as speculative but it seems at least probable that Winde and
Goudge were involved with Luttrell's rebuilding. The splendid staircase with its carved
wood foliage and dogs is also reminiscent of the work of Edward Pearce with whom
Winde and Goudge often collaborated. Comparison with Pearce's documented staircase
of 1676 at Sudbury Hall, Derbyshire[11], surely allows no other author to be considered.

On 20 December 1697 Winde wrote to Lady Bridgeman that:

> in ye Spring (God permitting) I am ingage to waite on the Duches of Norfolk to
> Drayden in Northehamptonshier & frome thence withe the D. of Powis to ye Read
> Castel in Mongomeryshire.

Powis Castle, a National Trust property near to Welshpool has late sixteenth-century
plasterwork and panelling but it is instructive to look for Winde's involvement in the late
1690s. The Marquis of Powis was a nephew of Winde's patron Lord Craven. He went

5   Drawing, attributed to Goudge,
c 1680 (Royal Institute of British
Architects Drawings Collection)

6   Drawing, attributed to Goudge, *c* 1680
(Royal Institute of British Architects Drawings
Collection)

into exile in 1688 and the Castle was probably in need of extensive refurbishing, in which Goudge may have been involved, after it had been empty for so many years. Verrio certainly painted the staircase ceiling, and the slightly later paintings on the walls by Gerard Lanscroon are signed and dated 1705. It seems likely that Winde's work was carried out for both the Marquis of Powis, and after 1696 for one of William III's Dutch followers, William Henry Van Nassau van Zuylesteyn, created the 1st Earl of Rochford.

In 1684 Winde had started to fit up Powis House in Lincoln's Inn Fields for the Marquis. There was also more work a year or two later for Lord Craven 'in a late building at Drury House'. Winde was then living 'over against the Earl of Craven's house in Drury Lane', and we know from his letter of 18 August 1688 that Goudge had worked there. What is surprising is the way Winde was able to attend to his business – however tardily – in time of national strife, and Goudge certainly journeyed forth unheeded. Writing to Lady Bridgeman on 2 October 1688 from Knightsbridge Winde indicated

> we looke evry hour when we shall march 'tis said the Dutch landing is speedily
> expected, but if it please God to bring me safe back it will be my delight to waite on
> Sr John & Yor Ladyp at Castle Bromwich, the draught of the Hall I will returne by
> Mr Goudge, who designes, I think, to sett forward on Monday next. . . .

When more settled times came Winde's activity as an architect had declined although Goudge did work at Chatsworth in 1696, receiving £155 for his work on the lavish Library ceiling.[12] Two of the last enterprises with which Winde's name has been connected were the advice he gave to John, Lord Ashburnham when building Ampthill Park, Bedfordshire, 1704–7, and the building of Buckingham House in 1705.

On 15 October 1706 Lord Ashburnham asked Winde's advice concerning the nature and manner of plastering the great hall to make it fit and proper to be painted by Louis Laguerre. It is doubtful if the plastering was done by Goudge, as his lament of 1702

7 Dunster Castle,
Somerset.
The Dining Room

8 Dunster Castle. Detail of Dining Room ceiling, with the incised date 1681.
This is similar in composition to the drawing shown in Fig 5

9   Dunster Castle. Detail of panel for the Dining Room ceiling, 1681

seems to imply he was ceasing his plastering work partly on account of the activities of painters such as Laguerre. It is not known whether Winde went on to employ Goudge's assistant David Lance, who in any case was to become even busier when appointed Master Plasterer to the Office of Works. It is not known either if he was the 'Mr Edward Goudge' granted a pass to go to Harwich and Holland in 1693,[13] and as yet his will and date of death have not been established. It seems however certain that by the reign of Queen Anne, the long and distinguished career of Edward Goudge, plasterer – 'the beste master in England in his profession' – was over.

Notes

1 Melbourne MSS, Bundle 99. Extracts from some of Goudge's letters are given in Historical Manuscripts Commission, *12th Report* (Earl Cowper) Vols 2, 3.

2 *Vertue Notebooks*, Walpole Society.

3 Probably Samuel Mellish of Doncaster, Deputy Lieutenant for Yorkshire who died in 1707 (H. M. Colvin, *A Biographical Dictionary of English Architects, 1660-1840* (1954), p 272.

4 Guildhall Library, MS, 6122, 1-3.

5 Earl of Bradford's archives, Weston Hall, Staffs, Box 76.

6 Bundle 99, see note 1 above.

7 Bodleian Library, MS, Gough, Warwickshire 1.

8 Ibid, Gough Drawings, a.2, ff 21-22.

9 RIBA, Drawings, Collection, IV/18(2); 18(4).

10 Dudley Dodd, National Trust guidebook to Dunster Castle, 1976.

11 John Cornforth and Oliver Hill, *English Country Houses: Caroline*, 1966, pls 280-81.

12 Chatsworth MSS, James Whildon's Account, pp 121, 123, 125, 135; Francis Thompson, *History of Chatsworth*, 1949, pp 56, 166-68.

13 *Calendar, State Papers, Domestic* (1693), p 37.

1 *John Soane* by Christopher William Hunneman, 1776
(Soane Museum)

2 *Philip Yorke, 3rd Earl of Hardwicke* by George Romney,
c 1784 (National Trust, Wimpole Hall, Cambridgeshire)

John Soane, Philip Yorke and their Quest for Primitive Architecture

PIERRE DE LA RUFFINIERE DU PREY

Of the properties recently acquired by the National Trust, none illustrates better than Wimpole Hall, Cambridgeshire, the whole spectrum of eighteenth-century decorative design. From a sumptuous baroque chapel to a chaste neo-classical drawing-room, Wimpole's brilliant interiors mirror the entire development of British taste of the period. Its outbuildings are equally diverse, though less well known.[1] Among them, the utilitarian structures designed by John Soane (1753–1837; Fig 1), form the subject of this article. The group at Wimpole, culminating with the home farm and its thatched barn, are rare survivors from the dawn of scientific agricultural technology that has attracted increasing scholarly attention.[2] A still deeper significance lies in understanding their source as part of a peculiar fascination with primitive architecture, shared by Soane and his patron, Philip Yorke, third Earl of Hardwicke (1757–1834; Fig 2).

The first encounter between John Soane and Philip Yorke occurred in Italy under circumstances unusually auspicious for the future growth of their common interest. They met on 28 January 1779, amid the massive columns of ancient Paestum where Soane was making measured drawings and Yorke was visiting the ruins. When Yorke wrote enthusiastically about 'the three temples of Paestum of the old Doric order',[3] he hinted at their brute strength and archaic appearance. In contrast to the adverse criticisms of most contemporary Grand Tourists, Yorke's remark that he found the temples 'magnificent', singled him out as a traveller of better-than-average powers of observation, although he had only attained his twenty-first birthday. The slightly older, academically educated Soane saw the baseless Doric columns of Paestum as 'exceedingly rude', but he immediately qualified that statement by placing them, as Yorke had done, in a chronological sequence that led to the more refined examples of Greece.[4] Clearly both men had exchanged ideas on the evolution of ancient architecture while under the awesome influence of the peristyles of Paestum. Apart from anything else, memories such as these tended to link in friendship an artist and a prospective patron like Yorke and Soane once they returned home to England, in 1779 and 1780 respectively. To be sure, Soane would not forget so likely a client as young Yorke, already the owner of the manor of Hammels in Hertfordshire, and next in line to inherit Wimpole and the earldom.

In the decade before Soane's additions to Wimpole, Philip Yorke employed him at Hammels to build a famous dairy, completed within a few months during the summer of 1783 (Fig 3). It may have been intended as a first anniversary present from Philip to his wife, Lady Elizabeth Yorke.[5] Here she reigned supreme. On one side of the building she and her friends might partake of teas in the so-called strawberry room. On the other side, directly opposite, she could supervise the scalding of the utensils in order to prevent the spread of harmful bacteria. And straight through the middle, in the dairy proper, she received milk fresh from the cow, in jugs which then stood on marble-topped counters to cool off. A natural system of temperature control, consisting of cold stone surfaces, cross ventilation, and the insulation provided by thatch, ensured the even rising of the cream to the surface. Skimming, churning, whipping, and even the tasting of the final product, could all be accomplished under one functional yet ornamental roof.[6]

3 *Left* Plan and elevation of the dairy at Hammels, Hertfordshire, 1783 (from John Soane, *Plans, Elevations and Sections of Buildings . . .*, 1788)

4 *Right* Plan and elevation of a primitive hut (from William Wrighte, *Grotesque Architecture . . .*,1767)

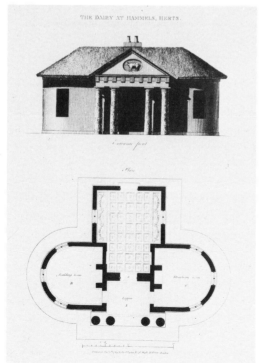

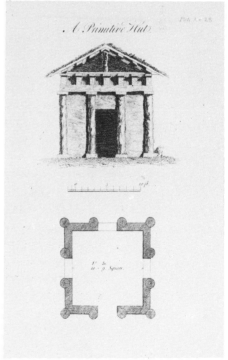

The fashion among aristocratic ladies of keeping dairies provided a useful outlet for prevalent emotional and intellectual cravings. Soane, in his account books, noted purchasing for Lady Elizabeth Yorke copies of Goethe's devastatingly popular *The Sorrows of Young Werther*, and one of Fanny Burney's novels.[7] Over her strawberries and cream, Lady Elizabeth could savour the touching stories of these books and thus cultivate the feelings of a woman of *sensibilité*. A well-established literary tradition, fostered by Goethe, Rousseau and many others, made readers, like Lady Elizabeth, prone to accept the notion of the basic goodness of mankind when in a state of nature. The romantic doctrine of the so-called return to nature called upon the pampered rich to renounce their artifice, in order to recapture lost purity and innocence. One should model oneself, the philosophy argued, upon the lives of those like the peasants who had not yet been contaminated. In this context, milk took on, in educated circles, some of the connotations still preserved today. Wholesome and unadulterated, it became by extension the preferred food of those like Lady Elizabeth seeking to emulate the virtuous ways of country folk.

The function of the Hammels dairy was announced by a medallion of a cow set in a classical pediment surrounded by rough-cast walls and thatch reminiscent of a cottage. Yet, thematically speaking, the purist, antique and rustic elements of this frontispiece blend together in a coherent way. The hitherto unpublished inscription on a Soane drawing, closely related to the dairy as built, explains its symbolism (Colour plate I). Soane described the columns as 'the Trunks of Elm Trees with the bark on & Honey suckles & Woodbines planted at their feet, forming festoons'. Then, quite unequivocally, he went on to call the design 'a Dairy in the primitive Manner of building'. This astonishingly clear statement of intent, would recall to Soane and Yorke the 'old Doric' columns at Paestum, and the legendary origins of architecture in the trees of the forest. Vitruvius, the ancient authority, stated that the first columns had been fashioned out of tree trunks. The eighteenth century enthusiastically embraced the hypothesis, because it confirmed the theory that all art had its roots in nature. The clumsiness of the Paestum columns mutely testified to their being one step removed from the beginnings of the evolutionary process. Similarly, milk and cottage architecture all tied in with the same search for basic truths.

Soane's phrase, 'the primitive Manner of building', announced his decision to penetrate beyond Paestum to the very source of classical architecture as described by Abbé Marc-Antoine Laugier. In the opening pages of his widely read *Essai sur l'architecture* of 1753, Laugier embellished upon Vitruvius by reconstructing the first man-made habitation as a cluster of four tree trunks with the branches entwined overhead to form a rudimentary shelter. This primitive hut, as he called it, should serve as the model for all future building. He went on to argue that infractions on the basic system, such as arches, pilasters and even walls, should at best be only tolerated.[8] Laugier's concept of the primitive hut caught on quickly in England where several varieties were illustrated in Sir William Chambers's magisterial *Treatise on Civil Architecture* of 1759. Soon pattern books followed suit. In 1767, William Wrighte introduced into his *Grotesque Architecture* a primitive hut inspired by those of Laugier and Chambers (Fig 4). Its inclusion in a book otherwise devoted to fairly frivolous follies condoned its use in the English landscape garden. Yorke and Soane may have been the first to take this idea seriously and carry it into execution. For the temple front of the Hammels dairy looks like Wrighte's polemical hut come to life. Only the little block of wood at the base of his

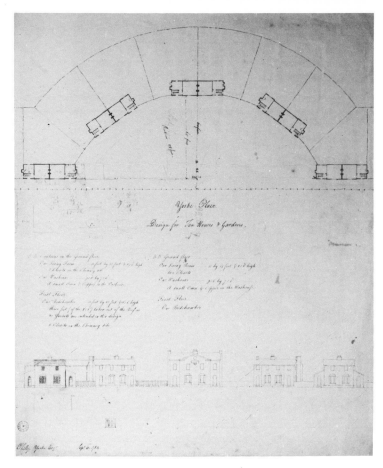

Order is absent, indicating that Soane boldly accepted baselessness as a characteristic of the Doric right from its inception.

Amid all this clamour for a return to nature, Nathaniel Kent sounded another sort of call in his book of 1775, *Hints to Gentlemen of Landed Property*. Addressing himself to the class of landlords like Philip Yorke, Kent wrote: 'Cottagers are indisputably the most beneficial race of people we have; they are bred up in greater simplicity, live more primitive lives, more free from vice and debauchery. . . .'[9] To the Yorkes, this doctrine must have seemed a logical extension of their interest in emulating the simple life. They did not need to seek out Rousseau's noble savage; he worked in their own back yard! Kent argued that good housing for labourers was in the best interests of humanity as well as increased productivity. What the owner laid out in costs for good sound accommodation – nothing fancy – he would recoup easily in a few years' time. As an enlightened young man of property, Philip Yorke could see the sense in this. Besides, the romantic, blood-and-soil appeal symbolized by Kent's writing, struck a chord of response in one committed to a return to the land. Kent coupled emotional advice with estimates, and practical ground plans to prove his points. Only his elevations were crude. An able agronomist, Kent had no pretensions to architectural ability. So, although his *Hints to Gentlemen* was the *incunabulum* of all the many cottage books that followed, Yorke would still have to look elsewhere for appropriate-looking exteriors.[10]

In September 1784, Yorke commissioned from Soane designs for cottages on the Hammels estate. Soane responded with a hitherto unknown drawing for an entire labourers' community (Fig 5). Yorke Place, as it was to be named, deserves to take its place among the pioneering model villages in England.[11] Soane called for five semi-detached cottages, each with its own garden plot, set along the perimeter of an elliptical green space. On plan, each half-cottage consisted of a main living area, with a kitchen

6 Plans and elevation for a cottage at Wimpole, Cambridgeshire, by John Soane, 1793 (Vassar College, Poughkeepsie, New York, Collection: Rev Elias Magoon)

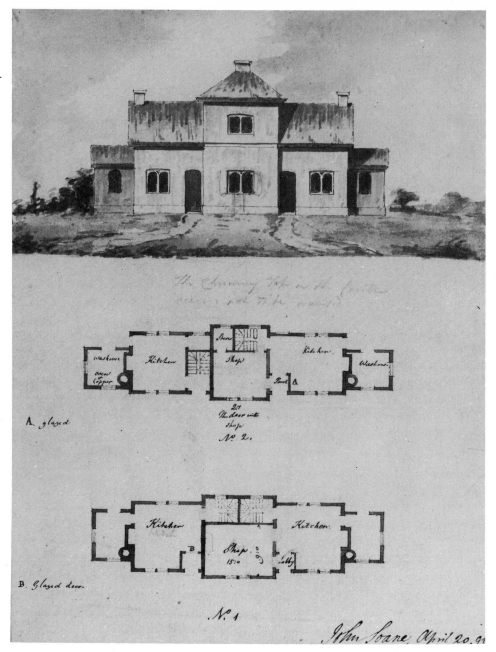

attached and stairs up to the bedrooms. Soane's fairly standard layouts recall almost exactly those of Nathaniel Kent, a copy of whose book the architect owned.[12] By contrast, the elevations suggest that Soane had abandoned the convention among model village planners to copy the regional vernacular building styles (for example, Milton Abbas, Dorset, 1773–79). Instead of rural quaintness, Soane's workers' houses have an honest dignity about them. Classical elements such as the central pediment, and the use of a modified Wyatt window-type on the ground floors, lend an air of up-to-date comfort. The severe interplay of geometric shapes amounts to a form of progressive primitivism in itself. Without resorting to the paraphernalia of tree trunks, Soane used the search for basic architectural truths as a springboard for the modern idiom, as Laugier had advocated. Soane artfully bridged the theoretical inconsistency that deprived the cottage movement of sincerity. The too-little-known Thomas Davis revealed this flaw in 1795 when he illustrated two types of cottage: the 'plain useful' and the 'ornamental';

Plate I   Plans and elevation of a dairy by John Soane, *c* 1782 (Victoria and Albert Museum)

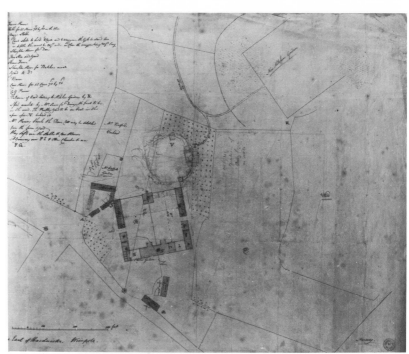

7   Plan and elevation for
a dairy at Wimpole,
Cambridgeshire, by John
Soane, *c* 1793 (Victoria
and Albert Museum)

8   Site plan for a dairy and the home farm at Wimpole, Cambridgeshire, by
John Soane, 1794 (Soane Museum)

as if appearances made no difference whatever to the inhabitants, only to the aesthetic
sense of the builder/owner.[13]

As an afterthought, Soane hatched in the windows of the last cottage on the left to
indicate leaded panes of glass. With this telltale alteration, he started to change the
entire mood of the drawing from geometrical elevation to one of poetic sentimentality.
In the amendments to the abandoned Yorke Place scheme, Soane set the stage for a
number of alternative cottage designs for Wimpole, that he produced in April 1793,
after Philip Yorke's succession to the earldom three years earlier.[14] The drawing illustrated here became separated from the others and soon crossed the Atlantic, where it
remains one of the few by Soane outside England (Fig 6). In the decade that had passed
since Soane and Yorke's working relationship began, they had decided to intensify
certain of the literal aspects of primitivism inherent in the Hammels buildings. Thatch
and leaded panes now run rampant all over the façades. And in Soane's book *Sketches
in Architecture* (1793), he described almost identical cottages with the familiar phrase
about tree-trunk columns smothered in creepers. Moreover, the Vassar drawing, though
it sticks to symmetricality, seeks by its receding wings to give the impression of a
picturesque rambling layout. A plan like this was actually executed at Wimpole in 1794,
to a different elevation.[15] The eventual inhabitants must have found their relocation a
trifle baffling. Here they were, being rehoused at considerable expense in a brick-built
replica of the same sort of ramshackled, wattle and daub dwelling they had traditionally
occupied. Presumably this irony did not strike Yorke or Soane.

Philip Yorke did not stop with building cottages at Wimpole. He seriously con-
templated another dairy for his wife. Most of Soane's designs for it continue the rustic
and primitive themes seen at Hammels.[16] One of the drawings that can be related
(Fig 7) shows a T-shaped plan, with the addition of some hen houses to the usual
dairying facilities. Comparing the Wimpole dairy design to the counterpart at Hammels
(Fig 3), a certain diminution of primitivism may be felt. All the elements of thatch,

baseless Doric portico and leaded windows reappear, without the earlier compact and functional organisation. The tendency to 'straggle out' the composition over the landscape, hence diluting it, has been noted before with the cottages as a characteristic of the picturesque outlook of the 1790's. In all respects, then, the Wimpole dairy and cottages were conceived as country cousins.

Although never erected, the dairy had a specific site designated for it, facing a grove of trees in close proximity to the Wimpole home farm (Fig 8). On top of the existing estate boundary lines, Soane sketched in pencil the 'agreed' position of the dairy and its attached poultry yard, at the points marked 'T' and 'V'. Lower down on the same sheet, where the public road to Old Wimpole is seen to narrow, Soane chose to situate his U-shaped farm-yard. By this time the farm, in its own right, had come to take on primitive overtones, thanks to the publication of Daniel Garret's *Designs and Estimates of Farm Houses* (1747).[17] Garret uttered sentiments reiterated by Laugier and Kent, when he traced the origin of architecture to 'the hermit's cave or Indian's hut'. Garret's evolutionary speculations, once attached to the farm as a building type, made it a natural vehicle for two apparently contradictory currents of thought: the rational search for improved agricultural structures, and the romantic back-to-the-soil ideology. Seen in conjunction with the Wimpole dairy and cottages, the farm would have formed a perfect rural enclave.

The site plan just discussed is not dated, but several other drawings are (Fig 9), and they help to pin-point the spring and summer of 1794 as the period of initial

9 Plan and elevations for the home farm at Wimpole, Cambridgeshire, by John Soane, 1794 (Soane Museum)

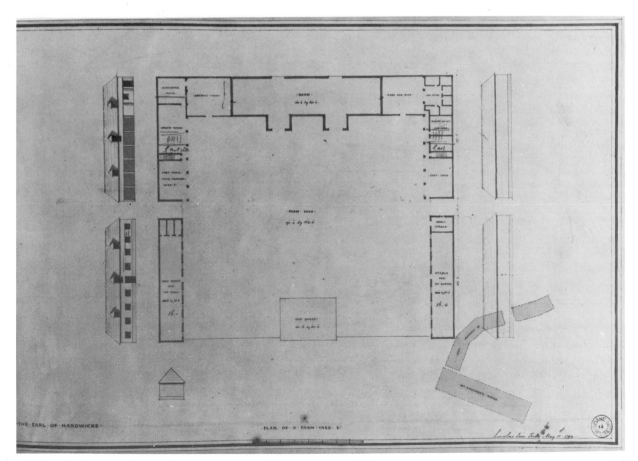

10 South-east range of
the home farm at Wimpole,
Cambridgeshire, in 1977

planning.[18] The farm-yard with its surrounding buildings remains largely intact, despite a few unsightly accretions. The north-east range (at the upper right corner of the plan) has vanished. The other three similar blocks set aside for cows, horses and carts survive. They all have brick bases, wooden siding and slate roofs with dormers (Fig 10). The open south side of the court, with a farmer's house in the centre, has completely changed, and is enclosed with low sheds and a higher brick wing projecting inward. Then, as now, the one-hundred-and-ten-foot-long barn dwarfs all else (Fig 11). With its two porch-like entrances, it occupies most of the north side. In terms of sheer acreage, its thatched roof eclipses all the other experiments of Soane and Yorke in rustic primitivism.[19] Naturally, with so simple a design Soane treads the thin line separating true primitivism from common building practice. But the barn would have gained in primitive impact from the artfulness of the dairy and cottages it was intended to compliment.

Independently, both Soane and Yorke followed their bent for the primitive in the years that followed. Though Soane never dabbled so extensively in the rustic style as he had when under the impetus of Yorke, one final burst of the same creative inspiration occurred as a by-product of Wimpole. It was what Soane called the barn 'à la Paestum', built at Solihull, Warwickshire, for another Grand Tourist acquaintance, Henry Greswolde Lewis.[20] This building, for a different client, linked the memory of Paestum, where Soane and Yorke's quest for primitive architecture had begun, with their realisation of how appropriate primitivism was to the whole class of rural structures: farms, barns, dairies and cottages. After the barn 'à la Paestum', such obvious manifestations wane in Soane's *oeuvre*.

Philip Yorke, for his part, continued to pursue his passionate concern for rural rejuvenation through architecture. As late as 1800,[21] he took the initiative to send Soane the plans of a Swiss farmhouse to study (Fig 12). The similarity between this barn and the one erected at Wimpole shows how folk-culture provided the source of inspiration to primitivists in their search for new directions in architecture. Yorke's heirs, later in the nineteenth century, inherited some of his enthusiastic idealism. A dairy was finally built at Wimpole in 1862, in a location close to that suggested by Soane and the third Earl. Now, with the recent acquisition of Wimpole by the National Trust, the tradition of enlightened estate management established by the Hardwickes, is likely to be resumed

12   Elevation of a Swiss farmhouse, anonymous, eighteenth century (National Trust, Wimpole Hall, Cambridgeshire)

11   South facade of the barn at Wimpole, Cambridgeshire, in 1977

after recent neglect. Mrs Bambridge, the last private owner, though she did so much to restore the splendour of the mansion, was unable to keep all the farm buildings in repair. Such is often their fate. The dairy at Hammels has long since gone without a trace, so have the cottages at Wimpole; only the home farm remains to remind us of the practical and artistic concerns that motivated both client and architect.

To picnic within the Wimpole farm-court today is an eerie experience (Fig 10). A deathly hush prevails in place of the hustle and bustle of men and animals. Doors swing in the wind, revealing empty stalls and granaries. Where the thatch has rotted away the sky looks through the roof of the barn. Hard-pressing though the economic facts are, it is very much to be hoped that funds can be found to arrest the dilapidation at Wimpole. Everywhere in the countryside, the landscape is blighted by buildings allowed to deteriorate, and the Wimpole farm complex is no more than a typical example. Many of the structures in question have years of useful life left in them for storage purposes, but are abandoned because thought to be unsuitable for modern farm machinery. The Wimpole group could continue to function in their original capacity, or be incorporated into a 'farm-museum'. Such working exhibitions of livestock and 'olden-time' equipment flourish with great success all over North America (like Upper Canada Village in Ontario, or Sturbridge Village, Massachusetts). As farming becomes ever more mechanical and industrialised, general interest in the fast-disappearing older methods grows – especially among the young. And, after all, the allure of thatch, latticed windows, rough-hewn timber, and the scent of honeysuckle round the door are as strong now as they were for John Soane and Philip Yorke nearly two hundred years ago.

Notes

1 Christopher Hussey dealt with the building of the house in 'Wimpole Hall, Cambridgeshire', *Country Life*, vol CXLII (1967), pp 1400-1404, 1466-71, 1594-97. His planned sequel article on the grounds and garden buildings never appeared. But for an account, see the RCHM volume for *West Cambridgeshire* (1968).

2 The state of research in this field has been published, together with a useful gazetteer, in John Martin Robinson's 'Model Farm Buildings of the Age of Improvement', *Architectural History*, vol XIX (1976), pp 17-31. See also the present writer's 'Oblivion for Soane's Cow Barn?', *Country Life*, vol CLIX (1976), p 84.

3 British Museum, Add MS 35,378, fol 305 verso, letter from Philip Yorke to his uncle Charles, second Earl of Hardwicke, dated 'Naples January 31st; 1779'. A recent summary of contemporary writings on

Paestum has been given by Michael J. McCarthy, 'Documents on the Greek Revival in Architecture', *Burlington Magazine*, vol CXIV (1972), pp 760-69. Yorke's travels, in so far as they relate to Soane's, I have discussed in my *John Soane's Architectural Education 1753-80* (New York, 1977).

4 Soane Museum, John Soane's 'Italian Sketches 1779' notebook, p 61. Soane never visited Greece but knew the Athenian variety of the baseless Doric Order from publications of the ruins.

5 Soane Museum, John Soane's 'Precedents in Architecture', fol 30 recto, has a plan and elevation of the dairy dated March 1783. In April and May of that year Soane exhibited a drawing of the dairy at the Royal Academy show. Presents of dairies are not unknown; see Paul Guth, 'La Laiterie de Rambouillet', *Connaissance des Arts*, vol LXXV (1958), pp 74-81, concerning Louis XVI's gift of a dairy to Marie-Antoinette in 1787.

6 The operation of an eighteenth-century dairy is discussed in J. Anderson's 'On the Management of the Dairy . . .', *Letters and Papers . . . Addressed to the Society Instituted at Bath . . .*, vol V (1790), pp 67-122. For the general topic of the eighteenth-century dairy mania, see Johannes Langner, 'Architecture Pastorale sous Louis XVI', *Art de France*, vol III (1963), pp 171-186. On the Hammels dairy in particular, see Dorothy Stroud, 'The Early Work of Soane', *Architectural Review*, vol CXXI (1957), pp 121-22, and John Summerson, *Sir John Soane* (1952), p 33.

7 Soane Museum, 'Soane Notebooks', vol X, p 29; vol XIII, p 10. Soane refers to 'Miss Burney's Louisa', but no such title is listed in the standard bibliographies. Probably Soane had in mind *Evelina* (1778), or *Cecilia* (1782).

8 On Laugier's primitive hut and its influence, see: Wolfgang Hermann, *Laugier and Eighteenth-Century French Theory* (1962); Joachim Gaus, 'Die Urhütte . . .', *Wallraf Richartz Jahrbuch*, vol XXXIII, (1971), p 22 ff; Joseph Rykwert, *On Adam's House in Paradise . . .* (New York, 1972). Laugier's *Essai* was translated into English in 1755, and his discussion of the primitive hut as a prototype is contained on p 11.

9 I quote from p 243 of the 1776 second edition. Kent's book was brought to my attention by Nicholas Cooper, 'The Myth of Cottage Life', *Country Life*, vol CXLI (1967), pp 1290-93.

10 Michael McMordie, 'Picturesque Pattern Books and pre-Victorian Designers', *Architectural History*, vol XVIII (1975), pp 43-59, provides an extensive bibliography of cottage books.

11 I find that Gillian Darley, in her otherwise comprehensive book, *Villages of Vision* (1975), was unaware of the Yorke Place drawing by Soane. But she does mention a slightly earlier, unpreserved Soane project for Allanbank, Berwickshire, from which the Hammels village derives.

12 Soane Museum, Architectural Library, 3B, has a copy of the second edition.

13 Thomas Davis, 'Address to the Landholders of this Kingdom; with Plans of Cottages for the Habitation of Labourers in the Country . . .', *Letters and Papers . . . Addressed to the Society Instituted at Bath . . .*, vol VII (1795), pp 294-310.

14 Soane Museum, 'Soane Notebooks', vol XIII, pp 11, 38, give the details relating to the examination of the site of Hammels and the staking out of the Yorke Place scheme. The following are the rest of the drawings for the Wimpole series of cottages in the Soane Museum: Architectural Library, Cupboard 22, 'Designs for Various Buildings by J. S. 1789-94', Item 25; Drawer 64, Set 6, Item 18.

15 Soane Museum, Drawer 64, Set 6, Item 19 ('Cottage at Wimpole Built with Brick Sept. 1, 1794'). The Vassar drawing was published by John Harris, *A Catalogue of British Drawings for Architecture, Decoration, Sculpture and Landscape Gardening 1550-1900 in American Collections*, Upper Saddle River, (1971), p 224, pl 170. But Harris did not connect the drawing with the designs for Wimpole cottages.

16 The verso of the sheet in the Victoria and Albert Museum also has a dairy scheme. Other drawings for the dairy at Wimpole are in the Soane Museum, Architectural Library, Cupboard 22, 'Designs for Various Buildings by J. S. 1789-94', Items 21-24.

17 On the literature and architectural development of this class of building, see Eileen Spiegel, 'The English Farm House: A Study of Architectural Theory and Design', PhD diss. (Columbia University, 1960). More specifically, consult Peter Leach, 'The Architecture of Daniel Garret: Designs from a Practical Man', *Country Life*, vol CLVI (1974), pp 694-97.

18 Soane Museum, Drawer 64, Set 6, Items 23-24, dated 5 July and 16 June 1794.

19 The RCHM volume for *West Cambridgeshire* (1968), p 223, claims that the barn was originally slated, not thatched. I see no evidence for this in Soane's drawings or accounts, and feel that the thatching tallies with the documented examples of its use in the cottages and dairy.

20 For the building history of the Solihull barn and an illustration, see Dorothy Stroud, 'Soane Barn', *Architectural Review*, vol CVIII (1956), pp 336-37 and *idem, The Architecture of Sir John Soane* (1961), p 81.

21 British Museum, Add MS 35,644, fol 30, letter from Soane to Yorke of 27 September 1800, acknowledging the loan of the plans for the Swiss Farm. Soane copied the drawings (Drawer 48, Set 4, Items 10-14). Three of the original drawings remain in an album at Wimpole.

John Fowler and the National Trust

JOHN CORNFORTH

The National Trust is a federation of places, and it is also a network of people: the range of both is equally wide. And just as occasionally a house of supreme importance or a work of art of compelling beauty comes into its ownership, now and again a key figure comes into its orbit and makes an outstanding contribution that is widely acknowledged, if not always as widely understood. So it was with John Fowler.

Eyebrows were often raised at the National Trust seeking the advice of an interior decorator, even one recognised to be a unique figure, and their questioning tilt was perfectly fair, not least because his work for the Trust was at times controversial. On several occasions in *Country Life* I wrote about houses where he had been involved and tried to explain what had been done and why, but those articles were not the place to go into the real nature of his contribution to the Trust; and, indeed, it is only after his death that it becomes possible to look back on his twenty years of work and put it into some kind of perspective.

1 John Fowler at home. He is seen here in a characteristic pose, giving orders to two of the boys who helped him every weekend in his garden at the Hunting Lodge

2 The Hunting Lodge, near Odiham, Hampshire, from the air. Built in the eighteenth century as an eyecatcher from Dogmersfield Park, it was restored by John Fowler, who also created the garden. He left the house to the National Trust in his will

John Fowler saw himself as the last of the *haute couture* decorators in England and he devoted most of his working life to the houses of people who understood, or at least accepted the concept of *haute couture*, even if they did not pursue it. He never set out to be a restorer or conservator in a formal sense, because when he was training himself there was no such concept as far as interior decoration was concerned. On the other hand, he had an exceptional sensitivity to houses, particularly of the eighteenth century, and he responded to many of their creators too. Also he had an extraordinary intuition and understanding of most of his clients and of the kind of background they needed for their lives. Thus his style was based on a synthesis of three main threads; artistic, historical and personal. When he began to do a little work for the Trust in the late 1950s, his country-house style with its cultivation of 'pleasing decay' represented a *beau ideal* to those responsible, because then the idea was that a house open to the public should look like one where the family had just gone out for the afternoon and that a fiction of a lived-in look should be created even in an uninhabited house.

It was not, however, as a creative decorator that he was approached. Rather was it that the Trust's staff realised the need for a special kind of advice on the handling of certain rooms, and they knew that he was the only person who could give it. He was then fully involved with Colefax and Fowler, and so it was as a favour to friends and out of a love for the houses that he was prepared to help over the revelation of old colours, matching them, working out complementary tones, and generally being asked to do the minimum for the least (and always insufficient) amount of money. It was all fairly tentative, because there was in the Trust considerable suspicion of interior decoration as such, practically no money and a great reluctance to tackle ambitious schemes.

However, there were increasing demands to see houses from a growing number of visitors, and that inevitably led to greater emphasis on their presentation and on the state of their decoration. Also, as a result of the particular methods of financing the transfer of houses through the Treasury, the Trust found it had to choose between doing more than it wanted straight away or possibly never having the chance again. Certainly this applied to Shugborough (Fig 3), which was the first big job that John Fowler planned and supervised for the Trust: little had been done to the interior of the house since it had been painted cream thirty-five years earlier, and so not only did it need repainting,

3   The Red Drawing Room at Shugborough, Staffordshire. John Fowler supervised the
redecoration of the room in 1962, as part of his first major work for the National Trust

but it needed colour and pattern to appeal to visitors. It was a new kind of challenge for the Trust, and John Fowler was the only person who could have carried it through.

After that his advice was sought with increasing frequency, as the list at the end of this article shows, but it was only because of the re-arrangement of his company in 1969 that he was able to retire from full-time involvement in Brook Street and combine a certain amount of work for his old clients with a formal association with the National Trust. The details of this do not concern us, but it is only fair to record how fortunate the Trust was to have the benefit of what was really his retirement: he accepted an honorarium and in return he had the personal satisfaction of carrying out work that had at least more chance of survival than most of his private commissions. He never had any illusions about the transitory nature of decoration, and so the Trust's houses provided not only a new kind of challenge but a hope of relative permanence for what he did.

Certainly that was so at Clandon, which was the most important of his Trust jobs. It was also the most demanding, because of the cold monumentality of the house and the lack of relationship between the grand, but rather sparse, Onslow possessions and the smaller scale and more exotic character of Mrs Gubbay's objects. However, not only did he create a remarkably convincing balance between them, but he managed to reveal the character of the house, particularly through his discovery of old colour and his introduction of new, and his work on the wallpapers, especially the green wallpaper of the 1730s in the Drawing Room (Colour plate II) and the Reveillon paper in the Palladio Room. One of his talents was an extraordinary ability to create a unity out of conflict and to turn what might seem disadvantages to advantage: in the Palladio room there was a tension between the Baroque plasterwork and the late eighteenth-century paper, but

5   The State Bed at Clandon. It was at John Fowler's suggestion that the case-curtains and rod, copied from an eighteenth-century engraving, were put up in order to protect the bed in the traditional way

4   The Green Drawing Room at Clandon before restoration. A photograph taken before the war.

6 In the Hunting Room at Clandon. Around the mirror, always in the room, John Fowler arranged some of Mrs Gubbay's Chinese birds on her gilt brackets. He made the festoon curtains, and the Brussels carpet, and the painted chair is one that he gave to the house

through his colours he was able to reconcile them; and in the Saloon (Colour plate III), where he found the blues and cane colours, he chose to keep the post-war curtains made of dyed blanket, as they were part of the history of the house. Such solutions were not academic, but then John Fowler was always empirical, and at Clandon he thought not only about the two main generations of Onslows and Mrs Gubbay's contribution, but of future visitors too. Thus he was both restorer and decorator.

Clandon was, I think, much more important in another way: it was there that John Fowler's gifts as a teacher became apparent. All who came were instructed in more aspects of detail than could have been covered by any other single person; the qualities of stucco in the Hall, shades of colour in the Saloon, ways of picking out a doorcase or a cornice, the point of case covers and the cut of festoon curtains. And it was not just decoration: he was just as interested in how the house had worked in the eighteenth-century, the contrast between the rooms of parade and the family rooms, how the house was warmed and lit, where the family ate and slept and where the logs were kept. Hours were spent peering and pondering in the penetrating chill, and then he would vanish to re-appear in triumph with a scrap of Georgian wallpaper or some byegone from a pile of junk. Often visitors longed to escape to the pub to thaw out, but now, looking back, I

Plate II   The Green Drawing Room at Clandon. John Fowler rediscovered and restored the green wallpaper of the 1730s, moving the state bed back to its original bedchamber on the other side of the Saloon

Plate III   The Saloon at Clandon Park, Surrey. The blues and cane colours were found by John Fowler under later layers of paint, but the curtains made in the post-war period from dyed army blankets were retained as being part of the history of the house

Plate IV   The Drawing Room at Wallington, redecorated with the advice of John Fowler in 1968.
Scrapes revealed that the walls had once been lilac blue with the ornament white but, as he felt this
would overpower the ceiling, which was not repainted, the colour was reversed

7   The Drawing Room at Wallington, Northumberland. A photograph taken before the death of Sir Charles Trevelyan in 1958

realise how vital that informal teaching was in opening the eyes of the staff and members of the committees who came to see the progress, and what a profound effect it has had on the way the Trust now considers its houses. He provided the basis for the development of a new professionalism, with the result that Clandon became a different kind of monument at the end. It became a statement about our knowledge of houses at a particular moment in time, and as it has turned out, the last chance people may get to see decoration of that quality carried out in a house. It seems inconceivable that the Trust will ever do anything as elaborate again.

While the work was going on at Clandon, attitudes were not standing still either inside or outside the Trust, and this is the hardest part of the story to put into focus. For a start, furniture history was taking a new direction and moving beyond the 'who made it' stage to 'why' and 'how was it used' and subsequently to the consideration of the arrangement of rooms and a new interest in the history of upholstery. Here the key figure has been the Keeper of the Department of Furniture and Woodwork at the Victoria and Albert Museum, Peter Thornton, and the influence on him of Scandinavian studies. It was inevitable that the approach that developed from this work should come to challenge the lived-in look, spreading out from a concern for the Victoria and Albert's direct responsibilities to a desire to influence the arrangement of other country houses, particularly those open to the public. Needless to say, this involved the Trust and a difference of view developed, the viewpoint depending to some extent on the age of the holder. Alongside grew up an increasing concern about colour and paint, and in the last three years Ian Bristow has been doing fruitful research in this field. Consequently, a much more academic attitude to interiors has developed.

John Fowler was interested in this new direction, and, indeed, the idea of detailed research on colour grew out of our own work together, but he was aware of the snags and he was by nature suspicious of what he considered academic theories. Consequently there were disagreements about approach, and his ill health made this more difficult, because he often did not remember why he knew something. It is never satisfactory to be told something as a fact but with no evidence, but, as I soon learned, it was wiser to accept the statement and look for the evidence; and the latter invariably turned up in the course of the next few weeks. Again and again his extraordinary visual memory was proved right, and, because he loved to talk, there were many opportunities to marvel at the way that he had trained himself to be historically minded. Although he was some-times called a scholar-decorator, I do not think that a happy label for him, because he never had the chance to order his knowledge, and, if he had, it might have stifled his flair. Rather did he create a personal synthesis out of his talent as an artist and his perception and memory of a great range of historical objects and places.

Most of his clients admired him and realised that his knowledge was unique, but few really understood his balance of gifts, and for years he worked in a degree of intellectual isolation that those of us who knew him in the last decade probably never even con-sidered. Certainly no one involved with the Trust could spark him off like Mrs Lancaster, who looked and laughed with him as no one else, or the late Lady Ancaster, a stimulating client and a generous friend, but instead he found a small circle of people who wanted to know more and with whom he could share his enthusiasm and knowledge. He was con-cerned that his experience should not die with him, and he found satisfaction in realising that he was having a profound influence on the Trust.

It was his response to people, his capacity for friendship, his sense of fun and his own forceful personality that made him a marvellous teacher, but it was odd how shy and unsure he could be. This made the first day of a new job decidedly sticky, but once he had established his position, new alliances would develop and new people would discover that white was not something that came ready-mixed in a can. At Wallington, for instance, he had a particularly happy and stimulating alliance with Mrs Geoffrey Pettit, and the success of this is fully apparent in the atmosphere they created in the house, combining extravagance and make-do and mend in a way that often brought out the best in him.

The Trust benefited from his gift for teaching and friendship in two other ways. He had a remarkable ability to gather round him people with special skills, which he would encourage them to develop, and then he would take endless pains to see that they had the right work. And such was his personality that he could persuade them to work under intolerable conditions. Many of these talented people as well as numerous firms with long traditions of fine work were thus introduced to the Trust. And as a valuable con-verse of this he was able to remind craftsmen of methods of work that they had half forgotten through lack of use and to revive them on jobs that he was organising for the Trust.

Nothing was ever too much trouble for him, and he expected – and usually got – that kind of standard from those who worked with him. But his standards were not confined to decoration. He was also fascinated by social practices, by housekeeping, and life below stairs, who did what and why; and he would talk for hours about what the disappearance of servants really meant. This was not wholly lost on the Trust, and the fact that standards of housekeeping and conservation are now going up is partly due to his practical inspiration.

Not all jobs were a hundred per cent success, and it would be wrong to claim that they were. Partly this was because the Trust did not always use his talents in the best way, partly because he found committees invariably frustrating, and also it was difficult to curb his enthusiasm on even the simplest subject. Also it should be remembered that he lived on cortisone for the last fifteen years of his life and had bouts of illness and worry. Moreover, the burning of his garden room with most of his records in 1965 was a crippling blow. After that I suspect he found it much harder to argue with himself about the true character of some of the things he was asked to do and to work out new solutions to problems: the demands of a large house a long way from home were just too great. He battled on, however, and right up to the end there were flashes of his old spirit, of his powers of observation, of his curiosity about history and of his sense of fun.

For many years he had admired what the Trust was trying to do, and during the last decade he became passionately devoted to it and concerned about its future. That was partly why we wrote our book *English Decoration in the Eighteenth Century*: it was a way of recording his knowledge as a first book for the Trust's Historic Buildings Representatives. But, as far as I know, he never discussed what the Trust would do about the decoration of houses after he gave up. Perhaps he felt that it should not try to copy what he had done and hoped that he had set it on its way, to find different solutions to the problems ahead, but he must have realised that those who had known him would continue to think about what he would have done. For them and for a much wider circle his spirit remains an uncannily compelling one: friends will go on talking about him as much as when he was only a telephone call away, and they will expect to find him in the houses where he worked as long as evidence of his touch remains.

John Fowler's work for the National Trust

This brief list is not intended as a comprehensive survey of all the advice given by John Fowler to National Trust Historic Buildings Representatives, but rather as a guide to the main redecoration schemes with which he was concerned, in roughly chronological order.

Claydon House, Buckinghamshire Decoration of the Pink Parlour, Staircase Hall, North Hall, Saloon, Library, Gothic Room and Chinese Room, 1956–67; the North Hall, Saloon, Staircase and Chinese Room redecorated in 1976.

Petworth House, Sussex Redecoration of the Grand Staircase 1962; the North Gallery and Beauty Room 1972.

West Wycombe Park, Buckinghamshire Redecoration of the King's Room, the Study and the Gallery and advice on decoration of the Tapestry Room, the Library and the Red Drawing Room, 1963.

Shugborough, Staffordshire Decoration of many of the state rooms, including the Saloon, Red Drawing Room, Entrance Hall, Dining Room and Bust Parlour 1965; and the Library, 1969.

Clandon Park, Surrey Redecoration or restoration of all the main rooms, 1968–69.

Wallington Hall, Northumberland Complete redecoration of the Staircase Hall, Gallery, Needlework Room, Trevelyan Room and Bathroom, and partial decoration of the Saloon, Library, Study and Entrance Hall, 1968–69.

Uppark, Sussex   Advice over a long period in the cleaning of all the main rooms including a minimum amount of decoration in the Parlour, Drawing Room and Staircase Hall.

Sudbury Hall, Derbyshire   Redecoration of all the main rooms, and advice on modifications to the garden, 1968–70.

Castle Ward, Co Down, Northern Ireland   Redecoration of most of the rooms shown to the public, including the Boudoir, Saloon, Hall and Staircase, 1969–70.

Blickling Hall, Norfolk   Advice on the restoration of the State Bedroom, 1969–70.

Attingham Park, Salop   Decoration of Lord Berwick's Study, 1971.

Temple of the Winds, Mount Stewart, Co Down   Advice on the redecoration of the interior, 1971.

Peckover Hall, Cambridgeshire   Preliminary advice on the redecoration of the Dining and Smoking Rooms, 1971–72.

Tatton Park, Cheshire   Advice on the repainting of the Entrance Hall, 1972–73.

Lyme Park, Cheshire   Decoration of the Entrance Hall, Staircase, Saloon, Morning Room and Blue Bedroom, and the restoration of the State Bed, 1972–74.

Montacute House, Somerset   Decoration of the Great Hall, Drawing Room, Library Ante-Room, Lord Curzon's Room, and the Long Gallery with its four side rooms (for the National Portrait Gallery), 1972–75.

Lacock Abbey, Wiltshire   Redecoration of the Hall, 1973.

Treasurer's House, York   Redecoration of the Great Hall and Court Room, 1973–74.

Erddig Park, Clwyd   Advice on the restoration of the wallpapers in the State Bedroom and Chinese Room and on textiles in the Saloon and Dining Room 1973–77.

Felbrigg Hall, Norfolk   Advice on the decoration of three bedrooms, 1974.

Ormesby Hall, Cleveland   Decoration of the Hall, 1974.

Fenton House, Hampstead   Decoration of all rooms on the ground and first floors, 1974.

The Assembly Rooms, Bath   Preliminary advice on redecoration, 1974–75.

Cliveden, Buckinghamshire   Advice on the paintwork inside the Blenheim Pavilion, 1975.

Dyrham Park, Gloucestershire   General advice on the redecoration of the Great Hall, Dining Room, Print Room and Display Room, 1976–77.

Juniper Hall, Surrey   Redecoration of the Drawing Room 1976–77.

1   Double-barrel sporting gun by John Manton

2   The spring-gun

Firearms at Felbrigg

D. H. L. BACK

Felbrigg Hall, dating from the seventeenth century, is situated near Cromer in the sporting county of Norfolk. Owned successively by the Wyndham and Ketton families, house and grounds were, with the exception of two periods in the nineteenth-century, kept down the years in immaculate order. The house is full of treasures and out-of-doors there is a sportsman's paradise, as may be judged from the extent of the Great Wood which covers no less than 500 acres. We know from the game-books in the library that in 1827 the bag amounted to 4,708 head and that the estate record of 5,383 head was made in 1834. One might expect that there would be a gunroom filled with sporting weapons, arms for defence and for settling affairs of honour, with all the necessary accompanying equipment. So indeed there must have been, and yet in an estate where so much has been cared for to perfection, what do we find? The following is a complete list.

A double-barrel shotgun no 4071 by John Manton. *c* 1802. Sold in 1968.
A spring-gun. Late eighteenth century.
A single-barrel sporting rifle, no 8433 by Charles Lancaster. Late nineteenth century.
A single-barrel target-shooting bench rifle. Late eighteenth century.
A blunderbuss by T. Cole. *c* 1670.
A musketoon by Major Simon Parry. *c* 1680.
A blunderbuss by Edward Bond. *c* 1770.
A pair of cannon barrelled pistols by Bunney. *c* 1776.
A pair of pocket pistols by Osborne & Jackson. *c* 1840.
A pair of unsigned pocket pistols. *c* 1840.
A service type percussion pistol. *c* 1850.
A Turkish flintlock rifle. Nineteenth century.
A tinder lighter by Henry Nock. *c* 1816.

It is pitifully small and the condition of the weapons is much to be regretted. However, by considering the various pieces that have survived, we can learn something of their purpose and so perhaps of their owners.

Pride of place must be given to the double-barrel sporting gun by John Manton of Dover Street, London (Fig 1). He was one of the best makers of his day, having been foreman to John Twigg before starting on his own in 1781. He made this flintlock gun in 1802 probably for a boy, the barrels being of 23 bore and only 27 inches long. It handles delightfully and is designed as side-by-side double-barrel guns still are today, except for the flint ignition and loading at muzzle in place of breech. In England until about 1800 double-barrel guns were the exception and the single-barrel had almost ruled supreme. There had been the feeling that two barrels were unsporting and a formidable case was made out that they were a danger to the user. In his book written in 1801, *Cautions to Young Sportsmen*, Sir Thomas Frankland sets out a most alarming list of the pitfalls and disadvantages. He concluded that a turnabout gun which has only one lock, the barrels being rotated by hand, was the answer for the man determined to have two barrels. This view was obviously not shared by the Lukin brothers, sons of Vice-Admiral William Lukin who took the name of Windham in 1824, having inherited

Felbrigg in 1810. The painting by William Bigg (Colour plate V) shows the four brothers with their gamekeeper outside Felbrigg Parsonage in 1803. Being young, they no doubt discounted any possible danger, when there was the practical advantage of taking two birds out of a covey instead of one by using a double-barrel gun. It seems most probable that one of the guns in the picture is the John Manton described. That there must have been powder flasks, shot belts, cases for spare flints, a turnscrew and much else besides in those days, is obvious, for we can be sure that those Lukin brothers shot whenever they could and probably with a touch of rivalry as to who should secure the largest bag.

Another item which we can connect with the sporting side of the estate is the spring gun which dates from the late eighteenth century. This weapon of 12 bore, belying its name, took a full load of powder and shot and was ignited by a flintlock in the normal manner. The lock and cover are now missing but it is shown in Fig 2, mounted for business. Along with other devices such as mantraps, one of which is still at Felbrigg, its purpose was to discourage poachers and others from trespassing, and to punish those who did. The trigger, instead of releasing the tumbler when pulled towards the butt as normal, operated when it was pulled by the cord which ran forward from the muzzle across a pathway. Loaded and cocked, the metal or leather cover was put down over the lock to keep out the weather and it would fire immediately the cord was drawn tight by man or beast. With the pivot mounted on a suitable block, it could be positioned in undergrowth where in its coat of green paint it was invisible. The elevation could be set so that the shot caught the intruder in legs or body as desired, and for traversing, there was the spring. This perhaps requires a word or two of explanation. In those days, ships-of-war had port and starboard batteries of guns on carriages capable of only very limited traverse through the gun-ports, and when it was considered likely that a ship at anchor would have to be ready to engage an attacking vessel a cable was run out from the capstan and secured to the anchor cable. By turning the capstan head and hauling in or letting out on the cable the ship could be traversed so as to enable her guns to bear, and it was this cable which was known as a spring. In the case of the anti-poaching gun, a thin iron rod was tied to the trigger which had a hole drilled through it for the purpose and passed through an aperture in the front of the trigger-guard and then through a metal eye under the muzzle. To the forward end of the rod which was curled into a ring, cords were tied and these were secured on the far side of the paths or gaps. There might be two or three of these cords covering the various approaches to a track junction. An intruder bearing against any one cord would tighten it, and on the same principle as the warship turned by taking in on the spring, the gun would traverse towards the line of the appropriate cord and fire down that line. The scear-spring must have been strong so that a good pull was required before the scear was released from the bent of the tumbler.

The third item of a sporting nature is the .250-inch breech-loading centre-fire single-barrel rifle by Charles Lancaster of 151 New Bond Street, London, which dates from the late nineteenth century (centre of Fig 3). It has a rebounding lock and the breech is opened by an under lever. The two leaf sights are marked for ranges up to 150 yards and it must have been used for shooting small animals and birds such as rooks and crows. It is unusual in that it has an oval bore, the oval twisting up the length of the barrel and serving as rifling. Lancaster invented this system in 1850 initially to overcome the problem of loading a rifle at the muzzle with a projectile which would take the rifling and not strip on firing. Taking the rifling imparted spin to the projectile whereas if the

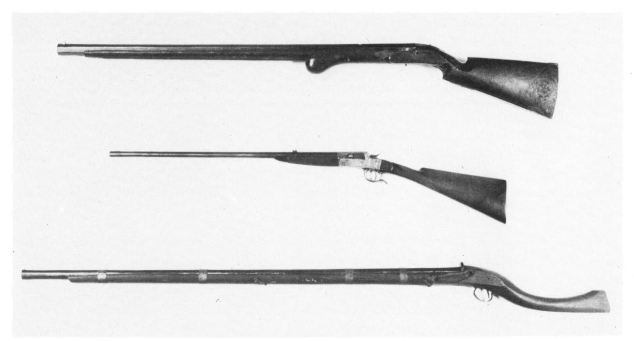

3 *Top:* A bench rifle for target shooting *Centre:* The oval-bored rifle by Charles Lancaster
Bottom: A rifle from the Middle East

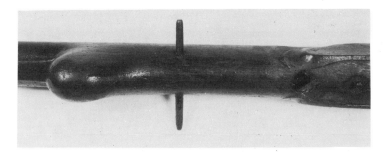

4 The underside of the bench rifle showing
the knob, trunnion bar and recess for
elevating screw

projectile slid over the rifles, its outer surface was stripped off and no stability was obtained. The two-groove rifle with its mechanically fitting belted ball had achieved success but at the expense of friction and increased recoil which made it necessary to employ only a fairly modest charge of powder. By changing the section of the ball from a round with a projection on each side to an oval, and making the section of the bore a corresponding oval which rotated through its length, Lancaster gave the projectile rotation and kept down the friction. Joseph Whitworth achieved a similar result in 1854 with a hexagonal bore and mechanically fitting projectile. Lancaster's system was successful and was carried forward to breech loading weapons which had brass cartridges holding elongated projectiles.

A very different type of rifle was almost certainly used for target shooting (Fig 3, top). It is without lock, trigger or guard and has lost its backsight so much of the evidence is missing. It may be added that it was completely broken through at the wrist and was insecurely joined by eight wire nails. Furthermore, so active had been the woodworms that the fore-end was eaten through into two pieces, and considerable patches of wood had been reduced to dust. After inspection, the present writer recommended that the wood should be burnt and only the nice barrel be retained. He was firmly put in his place on being told by the National Trust Representative that nothing made in the eighteenth century should ever be destroyed, and would he please restore it! To return to the rifle. It is a monster weighing 16 pounds, the single octagonal barrel which has an unlined touch-hole being of 10 bore, 37½-inches long and bearing no marks of proof. It is

53

rifled with 18 grooves. The dovetailed foresight is a ring mounted on a bar. The full-stock is heavily weighted with lead in the butt and has no provision for a ramrod. As may be seen in Fig 4, there is a large knob of wood on the underside of the fore-end and two iron 'trunnions' which effectively prevent the user from putting his left hand where he wants to place it. These trunnions are in fact an iron rod passing transversely through the fore-end underneath the barrel, and if placed in U-shaped supports would take the weight of the piece. Underneath there is a vertical hole of one-inch diameter passing right through the fore-end at the point of balance and exposing the bottom flat of the barrel. It is probable that this was made to take an elevating screw. The small of the butt is considerably inlet to allow an excellent grip for the right hand. The country of origin is indeed rather a matter of guesswork, but all these features point to a late eighteenth-century bench rifle of American or Continental manufacture, probably the former in view of the absence of proof marks. Target shooting, particularly in Germany, had for so long been a popular sport and much trouble was taken to produce an ideal weapon. In the eighteenth century, the matchlock survived so long because the lighted match ignited the charge without any jar such as that made by the concussion of flint on steel. The wheel-lock rifle likewise was retained because a wheel-lock ignited the charge just that much quicker than a flintlock, and so produced greater accuracy. Shooting with bench rifles was popular in America, and weapons were used which weighed up to 30 pounds or even more.

These four arms are all that can be mustered on the sporting side and of a case of duelling pistols which, quoting from *The Art of Duelling* by 'A Traveller', 1836, 'no young man should be without', there is no sign. There are, however, the weapons of defence, most varied in quality and purpose.

To begin with, two fine seventeenth-century barrels, one restocked, and both without their locks and some furniture. One gets the strong impression that not long ago a boy with a screwdriver took these weapons to pieces as far as he could. He unscrewed the screws that would turn, levered or broke off what would not, and took the bits and pieces, including most locks, back to school where perhaps they were bartered for treasures of a different nature. The only exception is the Manton gun which is in superb order and was disposed of by Mr Ketton-Cremer within the last decade. One of the two weapons is a high quality blunderbuss made by T. Cole in about 1670 and this is stocked in burnt maple (Figs 5 and 6). The other, a musketoon signed on the barrel 'Major Simon Parry', and of the same period, the barrel being similar in design to that by Cole but considerably bigger (Fig 7). The quality is equally good but the weapon has been restocked in beech by a local man. One can really enjoy these lovely brass barrels, each bearing the maker's mark and London proof marks, and both having the transverse ridge across the breech and engraving in the form of acanthus leaves, features typical of the period. As one would expect, they are belled at the muzzle, but not as has been so often stated, in order that any old pieces of metal which were at hand could be rammed down, or to make the pattern widely scattered. Blunderbusses handled about five drams of powder followed by a wad and a charge of swandrops – lead balls the size of a pea – held in place by a second wad. Some of these swandrops were far more likely to find their target than a single ball. The reason for the wide muzzle is rather a matter of opinion. Certainly it made loading easier. Another factor, very much applicable to shotguns was that gunmakers knew well that shot patterns are spoiled by the over-powder wad passing through them. This could happen in a gun bored tight forward which

5   The blunderbuss by T. Cole

6   Detail of the
blunderbuss by T. Cole

created friction between the shot and the barrel wall, slowing down the velocity of the
former. Boring the barrel tight behind ensured that the powder had to work hard from
the point of shot start and relieving the tightness forward allowed the shot velocity to
increase all the way to the muzzle. There seems no reason why this well tried principle
should not equally apply to the ballistics of blunderbusses. The musketoon is 47½-
inches long overall and is a powerful weapon – its use was presumably for the defence of
the house should the need arise.

The other blunderbuss by Edward Bond dates from the third quarter of the eighteenth century though it has the early feature in common with the two seventeenth-
century weapons of having the butt-plate secured by nails rather than by screws (Fig 7).
The brass barrel which has London proof marks and *EB* surmounted by a crown has a
reinforcing ring at the muzzle, and the lock which is of poorer quality than stock and
barrel is perhaps a local replacement of the original. It is poorly marked *E Bond* with the
B double struck and the cock is set out of alignment with the hammer. It could not have
produced anything approaching satisfactory ignition. Like the musketoon, the blunder-

7   *Above :* The
musketoon by Major
Simon Parry
Below : The blunderbuss
by E. Bond

55

Plate V *The Shooting Party* by W. R. Bigg (1765–1828). Canvas, 99 by 125 cm (National Trust, Felbrigg Hall, Norfolk)

busses could have been used for the defence of the house, but they would frequently have been carried on coach or carriage for protection against attack during a journey.

The mention of travelling leads one's thoughts to pistols and we have for a start an excellent pair of cannon-barrelled pistols by Bunney of London (Fig 8). They have silver butt-caps in the form of a mask which were probably made by Charles Freeth, and the Birmingham hallmark for 1776 (Fig 9). The boxlock action has a centrally placed cock and hammer which make it very difficult to take an accurate sight down the barrel. Each barrel has a lug on the underside so that it could be unscrewed for loading with the aid of a circular wrench cut with a key way to accept the lug. Unscrewing the barrel exposes the tubular powder chamber connected at its rear end with the touch-hole and cupped in front to take the 0.6-inch lead ball. This was very slightly greater in diameter than the barrel so that when the latter was screwed into place after loading, the charge was held snugly in place. This system had two decided advantages. Pistols loaded and set at half-cock in his saddle holsters by a traveller on horseback received a continuous jolting, and

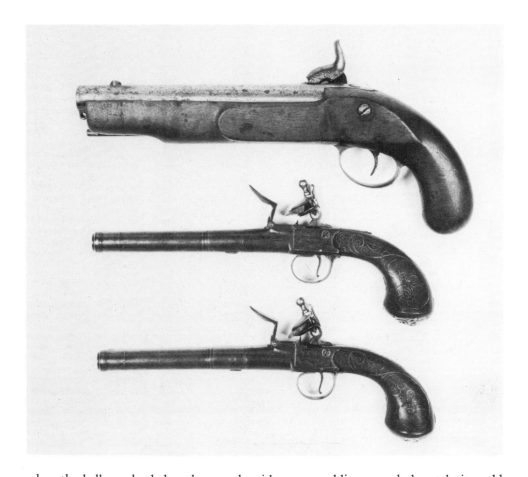

8 The service-type percussion pistol, and the pair of cannon-barrelled pistols by Bunney

9 The silver mask butt-cap on the Bunney pistols

when the ball was loaded at the muzzle with paper wadding or a cloth patch, it could shake loose. Falling to the muzzle at the bottom of the holster, much of the powder charge could follow it, and when an emergency arose and the pistol was drawn, presented and fired, there would be nothing but a flash in the pan. With an oversize ball in a barrel that screwed off this did not happen. The second advantage of the system was that the tight fit of the ball ensured that the shot start pressure was considerable and so when the powder did move the ball up the barrel, it drove it hard. The trigger-guards of these pistols incorporate very effective safety catches. With the spring correctly tensioned, it is impossible to fire with the guard in its backward position, but finger pressure moves it forward and in so doing the safety-block is moved away and the action is free to function on pressure of the trigger.

The pistols by Bunney are gentleman's weapons and so is a pair of pocket pistols by Osborne and Jackson (Fig 10, bottom). These also have barrels which screw on and off with a wrench, but they are ignited by copper cap instead of flint and steel. They were made c1840, proved at the Birmingham Proof House, and were carried in one's pocket for personal protection. Despite their small size, the barrel being but 1.8 inches long, they carried a dram of powder which gave them a formidable punch and they would prove effective at a much greater range than the few yards at which one could be reasonably sure of hitting one's target, since they are difficult to hold straight being so short and without sights. This pair in fact posed a problem as inspection down the barrel showed them to be fully loaded with the ball clearly visible. Ideally, one would simply unscrew the barrel, but after so many years this was impossible to move without the application of heat. Another solution was to fire them with a percussion cap. Holding in the hand with an unknown load is best avoided, and if the pistol is clamped in a vice one risks damage to the stock since there is no 'give' to absorb the recoil. The solution adopted was

10 *Above :* The pair of unsigned pocket pistols *Below :* The pair of pocket pistols by Osborne & Jackson

to drill the ball out from the muzzle end. Having unscrewed the nipple and removed as much powder as would come through the nipple recess, water was soaked into the powder until it would absorb no more. Even with this precaution, the task is un-enviable. One cannot be sure that the powder is all wet and when the bit has passed through the ball, the latter rotates with the former and still does not come out! However, with patience and care, shavings of lead and clogged powder were gradually removed and the whole chamber was cleared.

The second pair of pocket pistols, overcoat size, have 3-inch barrels which were proved at Birmingham (Fig 10, top). They also have percussion ignition, are unsigned, the quality is poor and they must have cost no more than a few shillings. Hardly what one would expect of Felbrigg! In the same category, though of more substantial construction, is a much larger copper cap pistol of about 1850 (Fig 8). This follows the military style with brass furniture, 9-inch barrel and a swivel ramrod, though this has gone. Main spring and scear spring are broken and the weapon has generally been greatly abused in fairly recent times. It also is unsigned. Having already referred to the problem of the ball falling down the barrel while the weapon was in the holster, it is worth mentioning that with a swivel ramrod it was sometimes the practice to leave the rod inserted in the barrel after loading. This held the ball in position and when the pistol was drawn, the rod fell out of the barrel but was not lost as it was retained by the swivel and could be replaced in the pipes when opportunity offered. This large pistol together with the unsigned pocket pistols are clearly servants' weapons.

The last of the firearms is a stranger – a middle Eastern flintlock rifle which is probably Turkish (Fig 3, bottom). The lock and ramrod are missing. The 44-inch octagonal barrel is rifled and has two aperture sights with a copper bead foresight, and it is secured to the full stock by four metal sleeves. Dating these weapons is not easy as they continued in use well into the present century, the design remaining unchanged. This one was probably made in the nineteenth century. How it came to Felbrigg must be conjecture – perhaps a memento of a tour to the Mediterranean area by a member of the family.

Thus ends the list of firearms at Felbrigg, so unrepresentative of what one might have expected to find, but none the less interesting on that account. On the other hand, one final item is exactly what one might have expected – a brass strike-a-light or tinder lighter. This one made by Henry Nock, one of the country's greatest gunmakers, is inscribed *Ex. Dono. A. W. Jany 6th* 1816 (Fig 11). It has been used and used until nearly broken due to the nose of the scear being chipped away. The candle-holder has been replaced, and given a new scear, it would continue to give excellent service if called on. In view of the fine quality and the inscription, it seems a fair conclusion that male members of the family used it themselves as a sure means of obtaining a light for their tobacco pipes from 1816 until the advent of the lucifer match.

'Mr Warren' and the Wrought Iron Gates at Clandon and Powis

EDWARD SAUNDERS

The properties of the National Trust can boast a number of fine works by the architectural wrought iron smith, but almost without exception the makers' names are unknown or, what is sometimes worse, loosely attributed to famous smiths on very flimsy evidence. Two of the finest pieces belonging to the Trust, the entrance gates at Clandon Park (Fig 8) and the Marquess gates at Powis Castle (Fig 5), have at one time or another both been attributed to the smith known only as 'Mr Warren', a figure almost as obscure as Huntington Shaw, who for many years was credited with the work of Jean Tijou at Hampton Court.

Starkie Gardner writing in 1912 was the first to reveal his name and it is from him that most of the attributions came. Sixty-five years after the publication of his *English Ironwork in the 17th and 18th Centuries*, is perhaps a good time to re-examine the evidence to see what new material has come to light in the intervening years.

1   The gatescreen at Clare College, Cambridge, leading to the bridge over the River Cam. The blacksmith Warren, who was paid for work at the college between 1713 and 1715, was almost certainly the same Thomas Warren employed just previously at Blenheim Palace, and at Hinwick Hall in Bedfordshire

'Mr Warren' was known to Starkie Gardner through one entry only in the account books at Clare College, Cambridge. The source of that information, a Mr J. R. Wardle, wrote up his findings three years later in the *Proceedings of the Cambridge Antiquarian Society*, in an article entitled, 'The Maker of the Iron Gates at Clare College'. Mr Wardle discusses the various entries in the College accounts books at some length, but the main facts are as follows:

> Warren (blacksmith) March 6 1713 and May 7 1714 in full for the Iron Gate next the fields . . . £35 0s 0d

On 20 July 1714 a college order was passed, 'that a convenient iron palisade for the garden, Gates for the Bridge Foot and entrance into the College shall be set up'. A further entry in the account book records that, 'Mr Warren was paid at several times from October 26 1714, to August 24 1715, £326 11s. 6d. for ironwork'.

The first question to settle is the identity of 'Mr Warren'. There are two contenders, John Warren and Thomas Warren, who both worked in the home counties, and who have both been claimed as the author of the work at Clare College (Figs 1 and 2).

The name of John Warren occurs only once in the accounts at Denham Place, Buckinghamshire, built between 1688 and 1701 for Sir Roger Hill. The name of the architect is not known, but might have been William Stanton, employed by Sir Roger as his mason contractor. The accounts in Sir Roger Hill's own hand are headed 'an acct of the money laid out in building my house at Denham commencing 1688 and continuing till 1701.' The total charges are given as £5591 16s 9d.

The claim that John Warren made the gates and screen that now stand in the garden (Fig 3) is not established beyond doubt. The accounts show that in all, four smiths worked on the house; Henry Truman, Daniel Byfield, Zach Godwin and John Warren. Byfield is described as an ironmonger and supplied goods continuously between 1690 and 1694. Godwin made only one brief appearance in 1690. Truman was paid £40 9s 6d in eighteen instalments between December 1689 and December 1691, and lastly Warren

3 *Denham Place, Buckinghamshire*, detail from an anonymous painting, *c* 1701. The gatescreen in the foreground has in the past been attributed to John Warren

was paid £21 9s 8d in seventeen instalments between April 1692 and July 1694. The gates are attributed to Warren on the grounds that the money he received coincided with a payment made on 3 March 1694 to 'Mr Osgood for ye figures upon ye great gates', but £21 9s 8d hardly seems sufficient for such a work. It would seem more likely that Truman, Godwin and Warren, were all employed to do general smith work and for some reason the payment for the screen was not recorded.

Nothing else is known about John Warren, though it has been suggested by Sir Niklaus Pevsner that he was responsible for the ironwork at Belton House in Lincolnshire, as William Stanton worked there under the architect, William Winde, a claim that must now be regarded as highly improbable.

Thomas Warren is a more substantial figure. We know he was responsible for architectural smith work, and more important, in 1712, when 'Mr Warren' was working at Clare College, Thomas was at Hinwick House, Bedfordshire, only thirty miles away.

4   The wrought iron screen in the garden at Hinwick Hall, Bedfordshire, attributed to Thomas Warren, who appears in the Orlebar family's building accounts between 1710 and 1712

5   The Marquess Gates, Powis Castle, North Wales, formerly attributed to Thomas Warren, and thought to date from about 1720

At Hinwick a building account book has been preserved in the Orlebar family archives, which show that between August 1710 and June 1712 he was paid in excess of £130 for unspecified smithwork.

The earliest entry, 'August 2nd 1710 Paid Mr Warren the remainder of his bill £33 14s. 0d.', suggests he was working at the house prior to this date. Of the remaining five entries two are marked 'home account', and one: 'Paid to Mr. Peter Slyford on Thomas Warren's account'. None of the ironwork has survived, but the fine contemporary screen in the garden of Hinwick Hall (Fig 4) may be Warren's work.

Perhaps more important for his standing as a craftsman, Thomas Warren was known to the Office of Works and used extensively at Blenheim Palace by Sir John Vanbrugh. At least four smiths were employed on the works at Blenheim, two of whom worked on the site at Woodstock. Warren was brought in from the outside and it was to him that the quality work was entrusted. On 3 December 1711, Sir John Vanbrugh in London wrote to the Clerk of Works, Henry Joynes at Blenheim, 'When I was at Blenheim last Mr Warren's man said he would write to his master to take London in the way thither, that I might give him directions what to proceed upon, but I hear nothing of him yet, he should write to him again for the ironwork for the stairs should go forward'. Joynes replied to say that he did not know where Mr Warren was or where he could be found. For posterity as well as Sir John this was a great pity, as a forwarding address would have solved a lot of problems, all we can say is that he was not a London smith. Mr J. R. Wardle in his article suggests that Warren might have been a Cambridge man as, at Clare, unlike the other tradesmen who came from a distance, he was not paid travelling expenses. However a close study of the Cambridgeshire records and wills has not brought his name to light.

So much is known about Thomas Warren that, on the strength of the evidence, the work at Cambridge must be ascribed to him, though it is to be hoped that some more definite proof will be found before long.

A connection between the Marquess gates at Powis (Fig 5) and those at Clare College referred to in the accounts as the 'gates at the Bridge Foot', came about in a most unusual manner. A few years ago Mr Raymond Lister's company were restoring the Clare College gates when he found upon them what he took to be the smith's mark. A short time after this when Mr Alan Knight was restoring the Marquess gates, he found in four separate places what he claims to be the same mark.

6 and 7 The marks found on the Powis Gates (*above*) and the Clare College Gates (*below*). The two are not, after all, stamped from the same die

Mr Lister has described the mark he found at Clare College in several ways. Seen as a symbol he thought it represented an anvil or a stake in a stand. Seen as letters he thought it might be H.E., but looked at the other way, it could be T.M. or even T.W., depending on how far one is prepared to stretch one's imagination. Now it is possible to see photographs of the two marks side by side (Figs 6 and 7), it is clear that the mark found by Mr Knight at Powis was not stamped from the same die as the one at Clare College. The Powis stamp is much the cruder of the two, and what appears as a bar under the W at Clare is seen only as a dot or a circle at Powis. Stylistically, the two gates have little in common apart from a sophistication in design one would expect from a master craftsman. Mr Knight confirms that at Powis both the smithwork and the *repoussé* is of the finest quality. It can be argued that the giant shells are out of proportion; perhaps the smith was the first to realise this, because as far as I know the motif was never repeated.

The gates at Powis are thought to date from about 1720 though so far no docu-

8 The gatescreen at Clandon Park, Surrey. Similar in style to the gates in Figs 9 and 10, which have also been attributed to Thomas Warren, though without documentary evidence

mentary evidence has been discovered to support this claim. However a thorough study of the Powis archives has still to be made, so proof may come to light. In the meantime the conclusion must be that the mark found by Mr Knight is not sufficient evidence to attribute the Powis gates to the Mr Warren who did the work at Clare College.

The attribution Starkie Gardner made to Warren of the magnificent gates at Clandon Park (Fig 8) is of a different order. As he cites no documents to support the claim it must be assumed that it was made on stylistic grounds. Starkie Gardner must have been uncertain as in a later book he does not repeat the claim. However he does point out the similarity between the gates at Clandon Park, and those at Devonshire House, Piccadilly, and the Kirkleatham Almshouses in Yorkshire. Yet such is Starkie Gardner's reputation that his original attribution at Clandon Park has now been extended to the other two gates, apparently without the slightest shred of evidence.

The most important of the gates in this group now stands at the entrance to Green Park in Piccadilly (Fig 9). Starkie Gardner tells us they originally came from Lord Heathfield's House at Turnham Green. They were later acquired by the Duke of Devonshire who moved them first to Chiswick House and later to Devonshire House in Piccadilly, but must have been set up in their present position by the 2nd Earl of Egremont, opposite the house designed for him by Matthew Brettingham senior (now the Naval and Military Club) in 1765; the Duke of Devonshire was earlier responsible for adding his own arms to the overthrow.

The second gate in this group now stands at the entrance to William Turner's Almshouses at Kirkleatham in North Yorkshire (Fig 10). In 1964 they were restored by Mr Downson of Kirkbymoorside, but he is not known to have found any marks upon them. All the evidence suggests that they were first erected about 1741 and moved from another location.

As for Clandon Park, the house was rebuilt by the Venetian architect Giacomo Leoni for Thomas Onslow in 1713–19. Pevsner says the gates (Fig 10) were moved to the present site in 1776, and suggests they came from the forecourt of the earlier house. If this is true they were set up before 1713.

The gates at Clandon have much in common with the gates Robert Bakewell made for the Derby Silk Mill, and show how two smiths can work their own ideas into what is fundamentally the same design. At Clandon and the Derby Silk Mill the arched form to

9　The gates leading into Green Park, London, from the north. Originally made for Lord Heathfield's house at Turnham Green, but moved first to Chiswick and then to their present position opposite Egremont House in Piccadilly

10　The almshouses at Kirkleatham, North Yorkshire. The gatescreen was probably moved here from another location in 1741

the gate is semi-circular, at Green Park and in Derby Cathedral it is elliptical. It is hard to believe that the two smiths did not know each other's designs. The probable link was the smiths' clients, who we know from other sources compared their designs and recommended their craftsmen to each other. Whether the smiths themselves knew each other we do not know, though some evidence is now coming to light to show that London craftsmen tended to live near each other in selected areas. One such colony was around Hyde Park Corner. In one terrace, Portugal Row, the rate books show were living the smiths, Jean Tijou, Thomas Robinson and Thomas Goff, the carvers John Nost and Andrew Carpenter and the painter Louis Laguerre. Such a collection of craftsmen living in one small row would seem to be more than coincidence.

The conclusion must be that there is still a lot of research to be done into the lives of architectural craftsmen and the contribution they made to the buildings of the seventeenth and eighteenth centuries. Though Starkie Gardner was somewhat precipitous with his attributions, most of which cannot be supported by modern research, his contribution to the subject of architectural wrought ironwork, after sixty-five years, has still to be surpassed.

Birds and Man on the County Antrim Coast

PHILIP S. WATSON

As far as birds are concerned, the world is shrinking every year and the coastline is no exception – reclamation, building and pollution take their toll and the unspoilt areas are often infested with humans seeking escape from the mess they have made elsewhere. But birds and man have been fortunate on the Antrim coast, so far. This area of Northern Ireland has been described and praised by writers, poets and naturalists for many years. Robert Lloyd Praeger, foremost among early twentieth-century Irish naturalists, referred to it as 'one of the most delightful playgrounds in Ireland' and both the Northern Ireland Tourist Board and the National Trust have not been slow to realise this. Served by a spectacular coast road that rarely loses sight of the sea, and with numerous small seaside resorts, the area is host each summer to an increasing number of tourists, holiday-makers, walkers and other people, all intent on making the most of the natural and man-made amenities. In these pursuits they are helped and encouraged by touring and other facilities while the National Trust owns or has negotiated access to considerable sections of the coastline and is increasingly linking these together with cliff-top paths.

However, the coastal strip is also the temporary summer home for many breeding sea-birds and numerous other species live here all the year round, well adapted to the

1 The north coast of County Antrim, looking east towards Fair Head. Rathlin Island is in the upper left corner and the famous Giant's Causeway in the lower right foreground

2 A black guillemot brings a butterfish back to its nest site in a crevice near Portrush in County Antrim. The bold black and white plumage changes to mottled grey and white in winter

3 A fulmar glides by on stiff wings. Widespread on most of the County Antrim coast, this large member of the petrel family is popular with bird-photographers and visitors to the cliffs as it shows little fear of man and can be approached quite closely. Nesting birds should not be disturbed and are quite capable of defending themselves by ejecting a foul-smelling stomach oil on to the intruder with surprising accuracy

often harsh conditions where land meets sea. How do birds and man, visitors and residents in both cases, interact on this coast, and is there a risk of disturbance to breeding birds from increasing human use of the area? These are two rather difficult questions that my colleague Jim Wells and I were asked to consider during a two-month survey of the bird communities in the summer of 1977. This was undertaken on behalf of the Northern Ireland Committee of the National Trust, with emphasis on their seaboard properties and paths from Cushendall to Portrush.

North of Cushendall, the coast varies considerably over the sixty kilometres covered by our survey. The eastern section faces the North Channel, a narrow stretch of water separating Ireland from Scotland by as little as thirty kilometres and characterised by strong tide-rips and deep water. The shoreline is rocky and low-lying but is backed by steep slopes which are closely grazed by sheep and rabbits. Rounding the north-east corner of Ireland at Torr Head, where the waters from the Irish Sea meet the Atlantic, the coastline becomes much more rugged (Fig 1). Lofty cliffs, dominated by the 210-metre high massif of Fair Head, are interspersed with occasional sandy beaches and this pattern continues west to the famous Giant's Causeway. Beyond this, the cliffs gradually give way to rocky coves, white strands and the golf courses of Portballintrae and Portrush.

The numerous sea-birds which nest on this coast feed during the summer in the inshore waters. Their distribution however, both on land and at sea, is not continuous. Few nest between Cushendall and Ballycastle except for small groups of herring gulls, shags and black guillemots (Fig 2). The fulmar (Fig 3), otherwise widespread on the County Antrim seaboard, is virtually absent along this section. The reason may well be the lack of suitable nesting sites, the shoreline being either too low-lying or at the other extreme so precipitous and smooth as to provide little space for an egg to be laid, let alone a bird to rest. It is worth looking out to sea however, because from June through to September gannets, Manx shearwaters and occasional arctic skuas pass by, either on migration or on their way to and from feeding areas. In addition to the birds, grey seals and brief views of the distinctive curved dorsal fin of pilot whales may complete the rewards of an hour or two's 'sea-watching'.

Rathlin Island, lying a few kilometres off Ballycastle, is the main sea-bird breeding station in Northern Ireland and it is also the province's only inhabited island, supporting a community of just over one hundred farmers and fishermen. Thirteen species of sea-bird breed here, numbering what ornithologists now refer to as 'order 5', which is from 10,000 to 100,000 individuals. Some have been counted accurately while others, such as burrow- and crevice-nesting puffins (Fig 4) and Manx shearwaters, are less well enumerated. Many of these birds are now under the protection of two nature reserves, one owned by the Department of the Environment (Northern Ireland) and the other by the Royal Society for the Protection of Birds. This surveillance does not extend out to sea, but to date the north coast has a relatively low intensity of oil tanker traffic and suffers little pollution, facts which can change with alarming rapidity if oil and gas interests so dictate.

Two much smaller mixed sea-bird colonies occur along the North Antrim coast, both on National Trust property. Sheep Island, a small steep-sided stack, contains Northern Ireland's largest cormorant colony (Fig 5) with at least 340 nests clustered around the edge of the cliffs on the perimeter of the island. Kittiwakes, razorbills (Fig 6) and guillemots (Fig 7) clamour on the ledges below and nine pairs of puffins provide evidence that the Trust's rat-extermination programme may be helping this

4 Puffins nest in burrows and crevices, thus making an accurate count of their numbers very difficult

5 A small section of the cormorant colony on Sheep Island, County Antrim

6 A group of razorbills loitering on the cliff-edge at Sheep Island, County Antrim. The birds are in full breeding plumage, the black of the chin and sides of the head moulting to white in winter

7 Three guillemots and a razorbill (*right*), showing the darker colouration and the heavier bill of the latter

bird to regain a foothold on the island where it was once extremely abundant. Facing Sheep Island, Carrick-a-Rede is joined to the mainland by a rope bridge during the summer months, which adds to its tourist appeal and tempts the braver visitors over to see the salmon fishery and the birds. This is the site of further busy aggregations of nesting sea-birds. With due care, members of the public can obtain excellent and often close views of the comings and goings of kittiwakes, fulmars, razorbills and guillemots, while the clear shallow water and white sandy seabed enable the observant to enjoy rare sights of the latter two species swimming under water in search of small fish.

Co-existence with man is well demonstrated by members of the gull family and the fulmar. Herring gulls and fulmars are constant companions of both commercial fishing vessels and anglers' boats offshore, where discarded fish, offal and bait provide a fairly regular food supply in contrast to the uncertainties of natural foraging. Although the fulmars are specialised scavengers with a taste for the oil-rich fish livers of the waste of human fishing activities, they also spend a lot of their time at sea searching for the larger plankton and surface-dwelling crustaceans that form their natural food. As these tend to be aggregated in favourable sea areas, so the fulmars and other feeding sea-birds are distributed unevenly over the sea, a fact which when combined with the ever-changing pattern of such distributions makes protection of the birds at sea a major problem. Gulls in general and the herring gull in particular have become much more dependent on man. The coastal towns and villages, where the human population is greatly boosted by summer visitors, provide these birds with a regular food supply at rubbish tips and sewage outfalls. The former are the favourite haunt of herring and some black-back gulls while the latter sites are frequently surrounded by black-headed and common gulls and kittiwakes. Studies carried out by David Melville on the food of herring gull chicks on the Skerries Islands off Portrush illustrate the use the foraging parent birds make of man's untidiness – amongst other items the diet included bread, meat, 'butcher's bones' and potato.

No mention has been made of the smaller birds – those 'little brown jobs' so perplexing to the inexperienced bird-watcher and the casual observer. A surprising variety exist on the Antrim coast in what appears at first glance to be an inhospitable habitat. Large trees are scarce and shrubs or other woody plants are scattered, except for gorse. But hedgerows are not far away, bordering the winding country roads and small, wooded glens are tucked between cliffs and cling to the less precipitous slopes. Stunted lime, ash, sycamore, birch, alder, hazel and willow provide both shelter and nest sites for many resident species. In spring, tired willow warblers, chiffchaffs, spotted flycatchers (Fig 8) and other migrants find time to feed and the summer insect life tempts some to remain and breed. In late June and throughout July, post-breeding flocks of tits and goldcrests move noisily through the thin canopy, some falling victim to the sparrowhawks (Fig 9) which breed in these wooded glens. Therefore, although many of the latter are tangled and almost inaccessible to man, they are valuable habitats for the passerine birds and also help to bind the thin soil on these slopes, while land-slips are quite frequent on the bare grazed sections.

Although facing the mainland of Britain, many of the woodland birds familiar to English bird-watchers are absent from these Irish thickets, indeed from Ireland as a whole. Woodpeckers and nuthatches are unknown, Pied flycatchers and redstarts are rare visitors and the tawny owl is replaced by the long-eared owl. However, there are

8 A spotted flycatcher brings insects to its nestlings in a County Antrim coastal woodland

9 A sparrowhawk attending its recently hatched young. A small number of these birds breed along the Antrim coast where there is sufficient woodland and cover

10 A pied wagtail at nest

abundant common birds such as robins, wrens, dunnocks and chaffinches while along the cliffs colourful wheatears and stonechats provide contrast to the duller hues of the skylarks, meadow and rock pipits and pied wagtails (Fig 10). Colonies of house martins on the cliffs illustrate the lack of respect this species can have for the name given it by man and they share their rocky habitat with such varied neighbours as fulmars, jackdaws and rock doves. When our survey was completed at the end of July, ninety species of birds had been recorded, many of them breeding. Taking the other seasons into account and including migrants and scarce visitors, the seaboard described above can offer the active bird-watcher 150 different species.

Land use on the coastal strip has its effects on the birds. Sheep grazing predominates from Cushendall to Fair Head, where some carcases provide carrion for the numerous magpies, hooded crows and occasional ravens. To the west, cultivated land extends in many places to the very edge of the cliffs. Flocks of rooks and jackdaws feed in these fields but the scarce chough prefers the close-cropped turf of the grazed slopes. Sheep and rabbits appear to be important components in the chough's ecological requirements, as are steep, inaccessible cliffs for nesting sites. Breeding surveys since the 1960's show that this species has declined markedly in Northern Ireland but the reasons are unknown, although much speculation exists. Rather than continued surveys of breeding strength, what is needed is a detailed study that would try to pinpoint the cause of the bird's present demise. Peregrine falcons and buzzards are two other species of special interest utilising the cliffs of the Antrim coast, and provide very good reasons for maintaining areas free from disturbance.

So far in this article I have discussed mainly the benefits, intended or otherwise, that the birds have derived from man. But birds are wild creatures, and they were here on the coast long before us; how we treat them is ultimately the outcome of our personal philosophies for nature conservation. Many birds react differently to intrusion by humans on their nesting (Fig 11) and feeding areas. Fulmars, for example, sit tight on their single chick or egg as people pass often within an arm's length of them, but the sudden appearance of someone at the edge of a cliff above a colony of razorbills or guillemots can result in a bird panic. These socially-nesting members of the auk family, if alarmed unexpectedly, take flight and the single egg can be dislodged from the narrow ledge on which it is laid and be smashed on the rocks or fall into the sea. The birds do not re-lay and such panics could have a detrimental effect on the breeding success of a colony. One should therefore approach such breeding sites carefully. This is an example where disturbance can be seen to have an immediate effect. Less obvious are the influences a picnic party or rock climbers may exert on a nesting bird such as the Peregrine falcon. Adult birds kept away from the nest for any length of time can result in serious harm to eggs and chicks which the offending visitor may never be aware of. Eggs may suffer lethal chilling, or on a hot day, overheating; young birds may be weakened through decreased frequency of feeding, or worse, leap from the nest if approached closely; predators may steal eggs (Fig 12) or kill chicks while the parent birds are absent or even be led to the nest by the trail the visitor has made. The list of hazards is long and a recent Canadian study of sensitive species (Fyfe & Olendorff, 1976) comes to a very sound conclusion – knowledgeable trespass on a bird's territory or no trespass at all.

Even if a bird is being disturbed it is difficult to measure this objectively. Results presented as numbers of nests deserted, eggs lost or unhatched and young killed can be exact, but they are too late. This does not mean that such data has no value, it can be

11 An oystercatcher with chick and egg. The shingle of the upper shoreline is a favoured nesting site and this species is liable to suffer disturbance during the breeding season as beaches become more popular and crowded in early summer

12 A herring gull steals a guillemot's egg while the parent bird is away. Opportunist predators such as this gull make the most of any disturbance to nesting birds

used to strengthen the case for future conservation. But it is much more beneficial, especially to the birds, when some measure of their reactions to various disturbing influences is achieved. However, the predictions based on such results tend to be uncertain and to be expressed using the phrases 'it appears that' and 'the data indicates'. This does not impress the hard-headed business and other interests involved in the development of coastal amenities and commerce. Therefore the increasing use of this coast for leisure and work demands a compromise. Areas containing species known to be sensitive to intrusion and which are not already under the protection of nature reserves may, with reasonable planning, be subjected to minimum disturbance while other sites which are less delicate may be utilised much more. One cannot expect the general public to be sympathetic to the needs of plants, birds and other animals if they are unaware of their existence and attractions. The coastline of counties Londonderry and Antrim is not without its field centres, interpretive displays, hides and other educational aids. As breeding success of the rarer species is improved and populations increase, it becomes impossible to warden all nesting sites adequately. It is here that an informed and concerned public can help in conservation, by reporting possible hazards such as interference with nests and illegal persecution.

This all adds up to a major responsibility on the part of those who own or control access to the coastline considered here, or any area where birds or other valuable natural assets are at risk. Over-simplification of conservation problems should be avoided at all costs. The Northern Ireland Committee of the National Trust is to be commended for sponsoring this preliminary work on the bird life of their north coast properties and I hope it will extend its concern to all natural history aspects of these areas, and to potential acquisitions. Thus in addition to having land held for the nation, it will not have been unmindful of its so-called 'lesser' inhabitants.

Acknowledgment
I wish to thank Mr G. Bond for permission to use his photographs to illustrate this article.

Bibliography
D. B. Cabot, 'The status and distribution of the Chough in Ireland', *Irish Naturalists Journal*, vol 15 (1965), pp 95-100.

J. S. Furphy, 'Rathlin Island', *Birds*, Royal Society for the Protection of Birds, (Spring, 1977), pp 22-23.

R. W. Fyfe and R. R. Olendorff, 'Minimising the dangers of nesting studies to raptors and other sensitive species', *Canadian Wildlife Service Occasional Paper*, no. 23 (Ottawa, 1976).

D. Melville, 'Analysis of Herring Gull pellets collected in County Antrim', *Report of the Seabird Group*, no. 4 (1972-74), pp 40-46.

R. L. Praeger, *The Way That I Went* (1937).

P. S. Watson and J. H. Wells, 'North Coast Breeding Bird Survey' (a report to the Northern Ireland Committee of the National Trust, 1977, unpublished).

High Victorian Horticulture: the Garden at Waddesdon

JOHN SALES

The Victorian desire for novelty and opulence was met by a revival of earlier formal styles of gardening embellished by new and more colourful flowering plants. Thanks to cheap coal, improved glasshouses and an increasingly skilled labour force it was possible to produce these tender plants in vast numbers, given the unparalleled resources at the command of landowners of the time. The garden at Waddesdon seems to express some of the best qualities of a positive age.[1] The whole history of its creation and development during the last quarter of the last century reflects a boldness and vigour born of supreme confidence, not only of the age itself but also of the ability to set and to solve the most complex technical problems in the shortest possible time.

Briefly the story goes that, eight years after his young wife had tragically died in childbirth, Baron Ferdinand de Rothschild came upon the site of Waddesdon when hunting. He resolved that here on this 'windswept and mis-shapen cone' he would build a home for himself and his family where, surrounded by the works of art which he avidly collected and in which he took such great delight, he could enjoy the company of his friends. In 1874 after inheriting a fortune from his father Baron Anselm of Vienna he bought the hill and 700 acres from the Duke of Marlborough and at once set about this task, employing a French architect, Gabriel-Hippolyte Destailleur, to build in the

1   An aerial view of Waddesdon, Buckinghamshire, from the south

2   An early photograph showing work in progress on the levelling of the top of the hill, before the building of the house

3   The circular approach drive at Waddesdon in course of construction and landscaping, showing the rail used for hauling stone and building materials as well as soil

style of the French châteaux.[2] The first design was rejected as too ambitious, but the architect was later proved right when the Baron had to extend the house, first on one side and then the other.

Baron Ferdinand also employed a French garden designer – Elie Lainé – for the design of the 'chief outlines of the park'. No doubt he and Destailleur agreed that the top of the hill should be cut off to create a level plâteau for the house and the formal gardens. An early photograph (Fig 2) shows many navvies at work with pick and shovel, cart and barrow, removing an average of nine feet in depth, over an area of ten and a half acres.

Another photograph (Fig 3) shows the extent of the earth moving, before the invention of the bulldozer, needed to create the splendid flowing landscape and subtle gradients of today. A fourteen-mile stretch of single-track railway line was constructed to bring the Bath stone right up from Quainton to the site. This was probably used, too, by Mr Sims the land-bailiff, who was responsible for the transplanting of all the many semi-mature trees, beech, oak and Horse Chestnut, that were planted, although most were moved on the 'Barron' transplanter. As well as a cable engine, a team of sixteen Percheron horses was imported from Normandy to provide the motive power. A gentle gradient had to be provided and the route of the track can still be traced from the main drive and through an area now known as Tay Bridge. The narrow valley is now a rocky dell spanned by a rustic bridge and planted with ferns and shrubs.

The main part of the house and the garden was completed by 1883 but work on the extensions and the aviary seems to have continued until 1888. No doubt new works continued in the garden too, especially the construction of the major rock features and the greenhouses. Although Lainé was consulted about the garden and the park, it seems that Baron Ferdinand, Mr Sims and the head gardeners, first Mr Bradshaw and then Mr 'Johnnie' Jacques, were chiefly responsible for the actual layout. His practice seems to have been to invite suggested schemes and then to plan something to his own taste.

It seems that Destailleur was also involved in the garden. He submitted a scheme for terraces south of the house based upon Le Vau's *grotte* at Vaux-le-Vicomte, which would have been set below the terrace facing away from the house.[3] But instead the main terrace was made much wider than the architect proposed, with the full unbroken rectangle being used for a parterre, not French but truly Victorian in character (Fig 1). A pool and Mozani's marble group of Pluto and Proserpine formed a centrepiece and fountain (Fig 4).

The wisdom of the choice of site with its dramatic views is obvious to any visitor. In general the layout of the garden consisted of an impressive combination of the formal and the informal. But I am not sure whether we would agree with its description in *Country Life* of 1898 as having in character 'the *simple* element of formality which springs from the architecture breaking forth into the free and natural beauties that surround'.[4]

The parterre is shown here (Colour plate VI) in pictures copied from hand-coloured stereoscopic transparencies of about 1910, compared with a similar view today (Colour plate VII). The effect was flamboyant in the extreme and must have been entirely successful in making the kind of impressive spectacle expected in gardens of great houses of the time. The main beds would have been changed twice a year, in October and late May, but the vases were replanted more frequently, usually four or five times throughout the year.

At all times the highest standards were maintained. Lady Warwick recounted in her

4 The marble fountain group of *Pluto and Proserpine* by Mozani in the centre of the parterre

memoirs[5] that she once arrived in a thunderstorm and was dismayed to find the masses of red geraniums had been beaten down by the storm. She happened to rise very early next morning and looked out to see:

> an army of gardeners at work taking out the damaged plants and putting in new ones, which had been brought from the glasshouses in pots. . . . After breakfast that morning I went into the grounds; the gardens had been completely transformed.

Today the effect is more sober. The beds were, and still are, purposely mounded up in the characteristically Victorian way, although this does tend to happen anyway to formal beds as the soil from potted plants is added each year. The layout continued in the same way until 1931 when a reduction in the number of gardeners demanded economies. From then until the time when Waddesdon was given to the National Trust the great parterre saw none of its traditional bedding out. Now the centre beds with their curving arms are again planted with geraniums and ageratums (Colour plate VII).

Comparing it with Versailles, the Waddesdon parterre is clearly not French in character. It has perhaps something in common with the heavy richness of Schwetzingen in Germany. But in reality both the design and the detail of its execution are entirely original and intensely Victorian and English. Some may prefer today's predominance of cool greens but there is no denying the drama and excitement of the original with its enormous specimens of *Agave americana* and *Cordyline australis*, exotic plants and brilliant colours. No opportunity for display was lost, especially near the house, and the geraniums were relentless.

The arrangement of bedding plants in the nineteenth century quickly developed into a convention, almost a ritual, with a set pattern and classification of plants according to their uses. The development of the twice-annual bedding system is usually attributed

5 Daffodil Valley, Waddesdon. On the left are groups of Horse Chestnut and sycamore and on the right Wellingtonia

to one John Fleming, Head Gardener to the Duchess of Sutherland at Cliveden, in the 1860s. Before this the main effort had been confined to the short summer display, using tender plants only. The major innovation was the use of overwintered plants, bulbs and biennials planted in the autumn after the summer display, to produce an additional spring display. Fleming wrote a little book called *Spring and Winter Gardening*, dated 1870, price 2s 6d, in which he suggested the use of, for instance, tulips and myosotis in place of evergreens in pots.

Plants were classified according to their uses in the beds.

1 *Edging* frequently a double line of dwarf plants using two different subjects.
2 *Groundwork* the main plants massed through the bed.
3 *Interplant* a second plant mixed in smaller numbers through the bed with the groundwork.
4 *Dot plants* large plants or plants of striking character used in small numbers.

Mr Ernest Field, who was for many years a gardener with Mr Alfred de Rothschild at nearby Halton, has recorded[6] that he 'once heard it said that rich people used to show their wealth by the size of their bedding plant list: 10,000 for squire, 20,000 for a baronet, 30,000 for an earl and 50,000 for a duke!' At Halton they produced 40,418 with a garden staff of sixty. It is highly unlikely that in either respect Waddesdon was outdone.

Another system involved the use of low plants to form patterns called 'carpet bedding'. This survives in the floral clocks and the bedded-out coats of arms of local authority parks. At Waddesdon there was a carpet bed in the south parterre and a fanciful 'basket bed' near the Aviary (Colour plate VIII).

Plate VI   The south parterre, Waddesdon, in 1910, from a hand-tinted stereoscopic transparency (Collection: Mrs James de Rothschild)

Plate VII   Part of the south parterre today

Plate VIII   The basket bed, Waddesdon, set above a pattern of carpet bedding, from a transparency taken in 1910 (Collection: Mrs James de Rothschild)

Plate IX   A similar bed today; behind the urn is *Ligustrum lucidum* flowering in September, Golden Yew and a glaucous form of box

Plate X   The former rose garden near the deer pen at Waddesdon, from a hand-printed transparency taken in 1910 (Collection: Mrs James de Rothschild). The flowers have gone but the statue on the right and the Wellingtonias still remain

The modern equivalent is rather less sumptuous but the remaining shrubs show the kind of subjects favoured for the borders and for general planting (Colour plate IX). Apart from the Spotted and Common Laurels normally associated with Victorian gardening, forms of holly, yew (especially Golden and Westfelton Yew), box (including the glaucous form) were widely used and have survived because they are long-lived. Privets (*Ligustrum lucidum* is especially effective in flower), lilacs, *Berberis* spp, Mock Orange, viburnums, rhododendrons, azaleas, weigelas, snowberries, dogwoods, and a wide variety of other shrubs were also used, many being planted as large specimens. *Hedera colchica*, together with Irish Ivy and other ivies; Butchers' Broom and *Sarcococca* spp, were added as ground cover. Quick-growing shrubs such as Double Gorse and brooms were planted in large close-planted masses at first but these have died out.

Many trees of thirty to forty feet were planted near the house, especially oaks, beeches, elms, limes and Horse Chestnuts and these were grouped effectively and with considerable foresight, as is shown in Daffodil Valley (Fig 5). They were associated with many of the currently popular and recently introduced conifers especially redwoods, spruces, firs, pines and Atlas Cedars. A group of Corsican Pines on the circular drive is especially effective in framing one of the many views out over the surrounding plain towards Bicester and Thame. The problems of ensuring continuity in a garden where trees are of such even age are considerable.

6 The North Front, Waddesdon, approached between Blue Atlantic Cedars and an avenue of oaks

The north front at Waddesdon has an impressive approach between eight rows of English oaks. Although planted as forty-year-old specimens they have failed to thrive because of the thin soil over limestone, exposed when the top was cut off the hill. This is a rare example of planting which was not totally successful and the policy now is to replace gradually with the more suitable Turkey Oak. From the far end beyond the fountain the full majesty of the concept can be realised (Fig 6). The north front also had its flower beds: strips of bedding surrounding large groups of Ghent azaleas and vases. Now there is nowhere else for the cars to go. Although not ideal for parking the scale is so large and the cars so well lost in the trees that they are at least acceptable.

The superb Aviary, also thought to be by Destailleur, was added in 1888. To see the birds and animals was an essential part of a visit to Waddesdon. Behind it is an enormous rocky outcrop (Fig 7), which from its style was almost certainly built by the famous firm of Pulham and Sons, who also built the cascade at Sheffield Park. This superbly contrived conceit, with its artificial cave, was originally intended as habitat for mountain sheep, but their pungent odour proved to be too close to the house. Two more sites were tried, each with its specially built rocky caverns, before the sheeps' final home was resolved, far below the kitchen garden on land not given to the Trust. The first area was then planted out as a rockery with a mixture of tender and permanent plants, pampas grass, ferns, palms and bedding plants.

7   The rock outcrop behind the Aviary at Waddesdon, originally a home for mountain sheep, and almost certainly constructed by the firm of Pulham and Sons

8 An early photograph of the wrought iron pergola and the Dairy at Waddesdon, entirely covered in Virginia Creeper

A normal Sunday morning entertainment for guests was to be conducted around the garden and Aviary, then down via the rock walk, past the rock pool bordered by Japanese Irises to the glasshouses (this rock garden was also planted out annually with Cabbage Trees (*Cordyline* spp), cultivars of *Agave americana* and bedding plants for colour). After seeing the glasshouses, visitors would be conducted through the rose garden and herbaceous borders to the model dairy where they would sample the cream, then perhaps to the kitchen garden. The dairy was rustic in appearance and covered with Virginia creeper (Fig 8). Nothing of this remains but the pergola nearby was rescued and now stands in the area near the deer pen beyond the Aviary.

This area was also planted richly with beds of flowers (Colour plate X), many tea roses together with more bedding plants, all in the 'gardenesque' style, a style much easier to recognise than to describe. Today the roses are no longer to be seen but this is recompensed by the splendid maturity of the Wellingtonias and beeches.

Returning to our tour: after lunch, in a procession of landaus, the whole party would drive to Eythrope, four miles distant, where Baron Ferdinand's sister Miss Alice had a pavilion and garden. If the Baron was the creator of the garden at Waddesdon it was certainly Miss Alice who developed it, and insisted upon the impeccable standards that earned Waddesdon an international horticultural reputation. Until 1922 when she

9 The former glasshouses and kitchen gardens at Waddesdon, from an early photograph

died it was Miss Alice who directed the garden work not only at Waddesdon but also at Eythrope and at her villa in Grasse, where because of her delicate health she spent each winter. When in England she always slept at Waddesdon because Eythrope was 'in the dangerously damp neighbourhood of a stream'. She was a generous but formidable lady who inspired and demanded respect from all. Once at Grasse she was said to have admonished Queen Victoria for stepping in a flower bed. But she became great friends with the Queen who liked her and admired her greatly for her exceptional organising ability; Miss Alice eventually named her villa after the Queen.

The glasshouses at Waddesdon were extensive, with about fifty separate houses or sections, with the domed palm house as the main feature (Fig 9). Until 1931 the house took the majority of the produce and the surplus was sold locally, but afterwards a more commercial approach was adopted with all kinds of flowers, pot plants, fruits and vegetables being sold through George Monro of Covent Garden.

A tour of the glasshouses began at the Vestibule, which was banked with flowers arranged formally. Malmaison Carnations (Souvenir de la Malmaison) were a great speciality both here and at Ascott and many new varieties were raised. The route led along the main corridor which was invariably banked on either side with potted plants. *Campanula pyramidalis* was a special favourite in Victorian times.

Leading off the corridor on either side were ranges of glasshouses each eighty feet long containing all sorts of pot plants. Here were gloxinias and there were African violets, crotons, euphorbias and of course *gloriosa rothschildiana*. Whole houses were devoted to anthuriums, cymbidiums, cattleyas, carnations and various pot plants. New varieties were selected by Miss Alice from new plants brought back by the head gardener who visited France and Germany annually.

Eventually one reached the Palm house which had an enormous tufa rockery and waterfall by the 'celebrated Mr Clapham',[7] then turned right into the show house (Fig 10) which had a winding path through well arranged, partly permanent planting among rocks laid by the first head gardener Mr Bradshaw; finally emerging into the formal rose garden and herbaceous walk which led to the fruit range. Other glasshouses were used for the production of tomatoes and beans over a long season.

Further ranges were devoted to the raising and overwintering of bedding plants. There was a seven acre kitchen garden, a 'reserve' garden for the raising of herbaceous plants and roses and even a heated span frame for the production of tender water lilies.

All this was presided over from 1892 by the head gardener, George Frederick Johnson, who held this post at Waddesdon for fifty-eight years. His father was a school-teacher and he went into gardening against his father's wishes. He first worked under 'Johnnie' Jacques, then went to Austria and to Miss Alice's villa at Grasse for experience. He was recommended by M. Gaucher, the head gardener there, to Miss Alice who appointed him head gardener, at the age of twenty-six years, to control this vast enterprise. He spoke three languages and travelled widely – and was held in great awe by the gardeners who always had to be seen hurrying when he was about. The garden was organised as a strict hierarchy into ten departments comprising between two and ten men. Members of different departments did not communicate with one another, and methods and reasons for the various practices were kept tightly secret.

The present head gardener Mr Ralph Saunders began at Waddesdon nearly fifty years ago. He worked under G. F. Johnson and was promoted by him to be Rose Grower at the remarkably early age of twenty years. In 1928 aged fourteen years he earned 10s a week, worked from 6.30 am to 5 pm with a half day on Saturday, and duty every third week-end. Last year he was very deservedly appointed an Associate of Honour of the Royal Horticultural Society.

10   The Show House, Waddesdon, with tree ferns, bamboos, tender bulbs and on the right *Campanula pyramidalis*, from an early photograph

Victorian horticulture possessed qualities never matched before or since. Undoubtedly it saw the highest point ever achieved in the craft of gardening, as distinct from the art and the science. At their best, as at Waddesdon, design and planting expressed the exuberance of the whole age. As Mrs Louisa Lawrence, the hostess and friend of Mrs Loudon said, it was 'all perfectly dazzling'.

Notes

1 This article is based on a paper given to the Garden History Society in November 1977. I am indebted to Mrs James de Rothschild for allowing me to copy, and reproduce here, some of her remarkable collection of hand-tinted stereoscopic transparencies and also for much help received from Colonel A. R. Waller, Administrator, and Mr R. Saunders, Head Gardener. I have also drawn freely upon Mrs de Rothschild's Introduction to E. K. Waterhouse, *Paintings in the James A. de Rothschild Collection at Waddesdon* (1967), entitled 'Waddesdon and the Rothschild Family'.

2 An account of the architecture of the house has recently been given by Sir Anthony Blunt in 'Destailleur at Waddesdon', *Apollo*, June 1977, pp 9-15.

3 Anon., *Gardeners' Chronicle*, 27 June 1885, pp 820-22.

4 Anon., *Country Life*, 20 August 1898, pp 208-11.

5 Frances, Countess of Warwick, *Afterthoughts* (1931), p 89

6 'Gardening Memories at Halton', *Country Life*, 11 October 1973, pp 1062-64.

7 Anon., 'Waddesdon Manor', *Gardeners' Chronicle*, 19 June 1886, pp 800-801.

1 *Compagne de Diane* by Guillaume Coustou
(1677–1746), marble, executed in 1717; height
178 cm (Israel Museum, Jerusalem)

2 *Compagne de Diane* by Jean-Louis Lemoyne
(1665–1755), marble, signed and dated 1724;
height 182.5 cm (National Gallery of Art,
Washington, D.C. Widener Collection)

Companions of Diana at Cliveden

TERENCE HODGKINSON

The Duc de Saint-Simon was, of course, exaggerating, when he wrote that Louis XIV had spent more on his beloved château at Marly than on Versailles; but it is true that during the last twenty-five years of the King's life, when the most ambitious undertakings at Versailles had been completed, expenditure on Marly continued at a very high level. An example of the scale on which projects were still being launched in his old age is the commissioning in 1710 of no fewer than ten life-size marble statues of *Nymphes de Diane* from ten different sculptors. Later, these statues were referred to as *Compagnes de Diane* and it is by this name that they are now remembered. All that we know of their origin is derived from the royal accounts.

The sculptors mentioned in the preliminary payments of 1710[1] are Dedieu, Flamen, Frémin, Lapierre, Lepautre, Magnier, Jean-Louis Lemoyne, Mazière, Poultier and Théodon. Further payments, some in the following reign, show that the series was later extended: two *Compagnes* by Poirier were executed between 1713 and 1715,[2] one by Cayot was completed by 1718;[3] a second *Compagne* by Flamen was executed in 1714[4] and one by Guillaume Coustou in 1717[5] (Fig 1). Cayot completed a model for a second *Compagne* but died in 1722 before he could execute the statue.[6] A *Compagne* by Jean-Louis Lemoyne paid for in 1726 (Fig 2) is now known to have been the one commissioned in 1710 and not to be a second statue by this sculptor as previously believed.[7]

Standing apart from these commissions are two much earlier references in the accounts: to a *Callisto, Compagne de Diane* by Flamen of 1696,[8] which was destined for Marly and a *Compagne de Diane* by Guillaume Hulot of 1699, which was left unfinished by the sculptor and eventually completed by his brother-in-law, Guillaume Coustou, in 1744.[9] Although Flamen's *Callisto* of 1696 was indeed delivered to Marly, it was transferred to Versailles in 1705 and may therefore have nothing to do with the commissions of 1710 and the following years.[10]

Combining all the references in the accounts we arrive at a total of eighteen *Compagnes de Diane* that were ordered between 1696 and 1722, of which probably fifteen were completed.[11]

The companions of Diana are attendant nymphs, portrayed much as is the goddess herself in the famous classical statue the *Diane de Versailles* (now in the Louvre), but without the crescent moon, that she wears as a diadem. The companions carry attributes of hunting, such as a bow and arrow, a quiver, a hunting horn and, in one case, a net for catching quails.[12] Some are accompanied by a greyhound. In the event, a number of the statues never arrived at Marly at all and others were there for only a few years, before being moved to another garden or put into store. In the aftermath of the French Revolution Marly was totally destroyed and, at the same period, a number of *Compagnes*, situated in other gardens, disappeared from the records. Several of these, however, have happily reappeared in public or in private collections at a later date.

At the last count eight *Compagnes de Diane* were known to exist, of which the most striking are the statues by Jean-Louis Lemoyne (Fig 2), now in the National Gallery of Art, Washington, and the statue by Guillaume I Coustou (Fig 1) in the Museum at Jerusalem (given by Baron Edmond de Rothschild). There is one in the Louvre (by Frémin) and one in the Hôtel de Rohan, Paris (by Mazière). Two are at Versailles (both by Flamen). One (by Poultier) is in the public park at Bolbec (Normandy) and the statue

3-4 *Compagne de Diane* by Claude Poirier (1657–1729), marble, signed; executed 1713–15; height 182 cm (National Trust, Cliveden)

started by Guillaume Hulot in 1696 and finished by Guillaume Coustou in 1744 is in a private collection. It must be nearly fifty years since the last identification was made, but there has always been a possibility that more *Compagnes* would materialise, not necessarily in France. The existence in the *Cabinet des Estampes* in Paris of fourteen early eighteenth-century drawings of the *Compagnes de Diane*, probably executed by the sculptors themselves,[13] strengthened the likelihood that more nymphs might one day be recognised.

4

Accordingly, the discovery of two *Compagnes de Diane* at Cliveden, which have been 'missing' since the eighteenth century, is not perhaps so surprising as the fact that no one identified them before (Figs 3–6). They are situated on the Lower Terrace and are placed rather unsuitably on the two central piers of an early seventeenth-century balustrade from the Villa Borghese in Rome. The signature *Poirie . . .* (for Poirier) and *Cayot* were observed during a recent programme of cleaning and restoring the sculptures at Cliveden.

5–6 *Compagne de Diane*
by Claude-Augustin Cayot
(1677–1722), marble,
signed; completed by
1718; height 174 cm
(National Trust, Cliveden)

The statue by Claude Poirier (1657–1729) is one of the pair executed by him in 1713–15, and recorded in the series of drawings in the Cabinet des Estampes (Fig 7). Both statues by Poirier were paid for in 1716. Although commissioned for Marly, both had been moved to the Tuileries Gardens by 1723, when they are described in an inventory:[14] one as holding two arrows in the right hand and a bow in the left, the other (the one at Cliveden) as bending her bow and having a quiver on her back. Claude Poirier played a considerable part in the sculptural decoration of the chapel at Versailles

6

and of the Dôme des Invalides, as well as executing a good deal of work at Marly. His nymph at Cliveden, while exceedingly pretty, is somewhat uneasily posed.

The statue by Claude-Augustin Cayot (1677–1722) has more authority. Striding forward, the nymph holds the leash of her greyhound in the left hand, steadying the bow with her right. The attitude reminds one of the nymph by Jean-Louis Lemoyne (Fig 2). As already mentioned, Cayot was commissioned to execute a second *Compagne de Diane*, but died at the age of forty-five in 1722 before it was executed. There is no

7 Early eighteenth-century drawing of the *Compagne de Diane* by Claude Poirier, now at Cliveden (Bibliothèque Nationale (Cabinet des Estampes), Paris)

drawing of a Cayot statue among those in the Cabinet des Estampes. When paid for in 1718 the completed Cayot statue had been placed in store in Paris. By 1723 it had been moved to the Tuileries Gardens, being described in the inventory as a *Compagne de Diane* by Cayot, having her dog at her feet on a leash, a quiver on her back and holding her bow with one hand.[15] Although his works are comparatively rare, there happens to be a marble group of Cupid and Psyche by Cayot in the Wallace Collection, which is signed by the artist exactly as he signed his Cliveden nymph.[16]

According to the inventory of 1723 there were in all, four *Compagnes* in the Tuileries Gardens, two by Poirier and one each by Cayot and by Mazière. After this date their history is uncertain. The Cayot statue is referred to in a publication of 1776 as being still in the Tuileries Gardens;[17] but this information could conceivably be out of date. According to unpublished evidence in the royal archives there are strong indications that all four *Compagnes* were moved from the Tuileries to the Hôtel du Grand Maître at Versailles in 1724.[18] The Poirier nymph holding the arrows was at a later date in the gardens of the château of La Muette, according to an inventory of 1746;[19] but there is no

8 Early eighteenth-century drawing of the *Compagne de Diane* by Claude Poirier, which was last recorded in 1746 as at La Muette (Bibliothèque Nationale (Cabinet des Estampes), Paris)

evidence that the two Cliveden nymphs were ever at La Muette. Indeed, the next firm information about their history is that they were purchased by the first Lord Astor for Cliveden early in the present century.

Lord Astor stated that he acquired them from the Château de Bagatelle. This small eighteenth century house in the Bois de Boulogne was inhabited from 1835 onwards by, successively, the 4th Marquess of Hertford, his son Sir Richard Wallace and finally the latter's secretary, Sir John Murray Scott, the residuary legatee of Lady Wallace's Estate. When the city of Paris purchased Bagatelle from Sir John Murray Scott in 1905, the works of art decorating the park were excluded from the sale and it is possible that Lord Astor bought the two Cliveden *Compagnes* privately at about this time. However, their former presence at Bagatelle has not yet been confirmed by an independent source. Lord Astor had already acquired the balustrade from the Villa Borghese, which dates from 1618, but he had not been permitted to purchase the two Roman antique statues, which formerly stood on the piers.[20] Presumably, the two *Compagnes de Diane* were acquired to fill the gaps.

Although the commissioning of this great set of sculptural variations on a theme was a most impressive act of patronage, the early dispersal of the statues spoiled their cumulative effect and the examples at Cliveden lose a good deal by their isolation. They remain supremely accomplished examples of the brief flowering of French rococo and, at the moment of writing, they are the only lifesize eighteenth-century marble statues in England that are known to have been commissioned by the French Crown.[21]

Abbreviations

Comptes	J. Guiffrey, *Comptes des Bâtiments du Roi sous le règne de Louis XIV* (Paris, 1891-1901).
Furcy-Raynaud	M. Furcy-Raynaud, 'Inventaire des Sculptures executées au XVIIIe siecle . . .' in Société de l'histoire de l'art français, *Archives de l'art français*, Nouvelle Période XIV (1927).
Réau GBA	L. Réau, 'Les Compagnes de Diane' in *Gazette des Beaux-Arts*, 6º période VII (1932).
Souchal	F. Souchal, *French Sculptors of the 17th and 18th centuries. The Reign of Louis XIV*, I (A-F) (Oxford, 1977).

Notes

1 Comptes, V, 432.

2 Comptes, V, 873.

3 Furcy-Raynaud, p 387. Souchal, p 86, no. 8.

4 Comptes, V, 874. Souchal, p 292, no. 62.

5 Souchal, p 138, no. 42.

6 Souchal, p 86, no. 9.

7 Réau GBA, p 144-45, and L. Réau, *Les Lemoyne* (Paris, 1927), p 34, no. 17; Professor Souchal very kindly informs me that new documents show Reau to have been mistaken on this point.

8 Comptes, IV, 8, 63 and 1184. Souchal, p 286, no. 35.

9 Comptes, IV, 479, 619, Furcy-Raynaud, p 86, Souchal, p 150, no. 79.

10 Michèle Beaulieu, 'La Diane d'Anselme Flamen et ses "Compagnes" ' in *La Revue du Louvre* (1973), p 83, suggests that the series of *Compagnes* may have been associated with a figure of Diana by Flamen of 1693, formerly at Marly and now in the Louvre. See also Souchal, p 285, no. 32, and F. Souchal, 'Anselme Flamen, "Natif de Saint-Omer", Sculpteur du roi' in *Gazette des Beaux-Arts*, 6e Période XCI, (1978) p 62.

11 Cayot's second Compagne was not executed, because he died. The statues ordered in 1710 from Dedieu and Lapierre, for which drawings exist (see below), are not mentioned in the accounts or inventories after 1710 and were therefore probably not completed.

12 By Flamen. Souchal, no. 62.

13 Ten of the drawings are illustrated in Réau GBA.

14 Ministère de l'Instruction Publique et des Beaux-Arts, *Inventaire-Général des Richesses d'Art de la France, Paris, Monuments Civils*, IV (Paris 1913) (compiled by H. Jouin), p 247.

15 See note 14 above.

16 J. G. Mann, *Wallace Collection Catalogues, Sculpture* (London, 1931), no. S22.

17 Fontenai, *Dictionnaire des Artistes* (Paris, 1776), I, p 342. Cayot's works are said to include 'une des compagnes de Diane, en marbre, dans le jardin des Thuileries'.

18 Archives nationales, o¹ 2300, fol. 52 vº. This information was very kindly supplied to me by Miss Betsy Rosasco.

19 An inventory of the statues in the garden of La Muette dated 1746 is published in Société de l'Histoire de l'art français, *Nouvelles Archives*, 3e série, VIII (1892), p 358-68.

20 P. della Pergola, *Villa Borghese* (Rome, 1962) p 79, note on pl 32.

21 Of the fifteen *Compagnes* which were probably completed, five have not yet been identified and might still exist. They are by Anselme Flamen (Souchal, no. 63), Pierre Lepautre, Philippe Magnier (drawing Réau GBA Fig 15), Claude Poirier (Fig 8 above), and Jean-Baptiste Théodon (finished by Benoît Massou).

Thomas Hardy and Stourhead

ROGER ALMA

> Thank you so much for your very kind letter. It will make a great difference to me to know that you are at the unveiling – I shall *know* that there are two there who cared for *him* for *himself*, & for the spirit that produced his work. Others will be there for various reasons – but you for friendship & affection. I so often think of you. Your friendship is indeed the brightest spot in my life.

The letter from which this extract is taken, sent from Max Gate, Dorchester, to Lady Hoare of Stourhead, on 29 August 1931, by Florence Hardy, second wife of the great novelist and poet, is one of the last of a long and fascinating correspondence between the Hardys and Lady Hoare. None of the many letters is without interest. They reflect the character of the writers, and the events and emotions of their lives, recording moments of happiness, and some deep sadnesses.

The occasion for Florence's letter was the unveiling of the statue of Thomas Hardy that can today be seen on the outskirts of Dorchester, looking out over his beloved Wessex. It was fitting that Lady Hoare should be there, because of her love and admiration of Hardy, and typical of her, in her relations with him at least, that she did not intrude upon the occasion, but remained discreetly in the background. Florence later wrote, on 7 September, 'I felt you were there, and I thought I saw your face'. The event marked the end of a long and warm friendship. Only one or two letters from Florence appear to have been written subsequently. The mainspring of her life seems to have been broken with her husband's death and the publication of the second volume of the biography that she wrote in conjunction with him. She wrote on 7 September, 'I feel now as if there had been a general "wind up", & that everything that mattered was ended'. Only half of her last letter to Lady Hoare has been preserved, tucked in a copy of a limited edition of Hardy's early novel, *An Indiscretion in the Life of an Heiress*, in the library at Stourhead, a letter apparently written in 1934, expressing to Lady Hoare gratitude and affection for their years of friendship. Florence died in 1937, and Lady Hoare ten years later, on the same day as her husband.

The story begins, however, many years before, in 1910, before Florence's marriage to Hardy. Lady Hoare (1861–1947), born Alda Weston, and the wife of Sir Henry Hoare, Bart, who most generously gave Stourhead to the National Trust in 1946, was a woman of considerable literary interests. Her own extensive 'boudoir library' included works by Tennyson, Wordsworth, Lindsay Gordon, Lord Chesterfield, Evelyn, Leigh Hunt, Jowett, Blake, Verlaine, Eliot, Fielding, Defoe, books on the Koran, Wagner, and so on. She subscribed to a number of literary periodicals, including the *Revue de Paris*, *Mercure de France* and *Revue des Revues*, and she made commonplace books of extracts from her favourite authors, which she called *Varia*, and in which are to be found passages from Jowett, Voltaire, Swinburne, Prior, Balzac, Boulanger, Gautier, Rousseau, Conrad, Lamartine, Browning, Henley and others. But the greatest literary passion of her life was Thomas Hardy, and the main library at Stourhead contains a valuable collection of autographed first editions of his works. In many of these books are still to be found notes and letters from Hardy and his second wife, Florence, written to Lady Hoare over the years of their friendship. Nearly all of the books are carefully annotated. Many of the notes simply identify the places mentioned in stories and poems, following Hermann Lea's *Thomas Hardy's Wessex* (1913), but sometimes more personal

1 J. M. Barrie unveiling the Hardy Memorial at Dorchester in 1931 (Dorset County Museum)

responses are recorded, by underlining and marginal comment. Also in the books are kept reviews of Hardy's works, cut from newspapers and magazines by Lady Hoare. Some of the material has now been removed, and is in safe-keeping at the Wiltshire County Record Office at Trowbridge, together with other letters by Thomas Hardy, Emma Lavinia Hardy, his first wife, and Florence Emily Hardy. A few letters by Lady Hoare, mainly to Emma, are kept at the Dorset County Museum in Dorchester, though unfortunately the bulk of her letters to the Hardys cannot be traced.

Lady Hoare seems to have first written to Hardy early in 1910, asking the author if he would autograph a copy of *Far From the Madding Crowd*. Hardy replied on 10 February, promising to sign the book and return it. The book, which is still in the Stourhead Library, has a note by Lady Hoare, written many years later in 1925, that 'this letter was the beginning of my friendship with a great poet and novelist, which was to prove one of the greatest and most valued, interest and happiness [sic]'. The friendship is little mentioned in the standard biographies of Hardy, with the exception of two entries in the biography by Florence Hardy herself, originally published in two volumes and now available as *The Life of Thomas Hardy, 1840–1928*. It seems, nevertheless, to have been an important one to the Hardys as well as to Lady Hoare.

The correspondence was at first taken up by Hardy's first wife, Emma. The unhappiness of the later years of this marriage is well known, and is partly revealed in the single letter that Lady Hoare appears to have kept of several that were written. The letter, now at Trowbridge, was written on 24 April 1910, to Lady Hoare at Bath, where

2 *Lady (Alda) Hoare* (1861–1947) by A. S. Stoppolini, 1898. Canvas 135 by 80 cm (National Trust, Stourhead, Wiltshire)

she was 'taking the cure'. The letter is rambling, amusing, interesting, and sad. Emma dismisses Lady Hoare's praise of her husband's work:

> My husband's books have not the same kind of interest for me, as for others. I knew every word of the *first* edition – in MS. sitting by his side – etc etc – so long ago, & so much endured since – in this town in which I have been *unhappy*, that they are bound to be different to me!

And later she comments that, as Hardy is away for a few days,

> I am ensconsing myself in the study in *his* big chair foraging – he keeps me *out* usually – as *never* formerly – ah well! I have my private opinion of men in general & of him in particular. . . .

The reader is reminded that, according to Sir Newman Flower's *Just As It Happened* (1950), Hardy had an outside staircase built so he might ascend to his study without going through the house. Emma's letter ends with an outburst against men in public positions, a reminder of her interest in the Women's Suffrage Movement.

Lady Hoare's letters of this period can be seen in Dorchester. Her tact in replying to Emma's outbursts is considerable, but she also defends Hardy's novels and asserts her own view of men. Her letters are written with a broad-nibbed pen. The hand-writing is bold and vigorous, suggesting a strong and impulsive character, an impression that is confirmed by the portrait of her in the hall at Stourhead. She evidently wrote quickly,

4 *Emma Lavinia Hardy* (d 1910), by an
unknown artist. Canvas 60 by 89 cm.
Thomas Hardy's first wife (Dorset County
Museum)

3 *Thomas Hardy* (1840-1928), by
William Strang, RA, 1919. Pencil drawing
30.4 by 25.4 cm (National Portrait Gallery)

covering side after side with large and flowing script. She praises one of Emma's poems,
which was apparently written after seeing the spring flowers at Stourhead, on a visit
before she knew the Hoares. She speaks of her reading, and her love of Swinburne,
Flaubert's *Madame Bovary*, and Hardy's *Jude the Obscure*, none of which was likely to
find sympathy with Emma, certainly not the last, which she asked her husband not to
publish! Lady Hoare responds amusingly to a reference made to an attack on Velasquez's
Venus in the National Gallery:

> 'Oh! by the way!!' wrote Lady Hoare, 'I *do* rejoice, at this business, over the
> Velasquez (?) Venus – I, always, hated *that* picture! – and I quite agree with Lord
> Wemyss: 'If it is Velasquez (?) it is very bad' –! If any woman were shaped like that,
> she should have been *shot*. . . .' [The punctuation is characteristic.]

Her letters also reveal her deep love of the countryside, where she walked with her dog,
'10, 12 to 13 miles every afternoon', and in particular her love of the gardens of Stourhead, and her willingness to share them with tourists, of whom her husband was a little
less tolerant, though with good humour. On 2 September 1911, she wrote:

5   Max Gate, Dorchester. The house designed by Thomas Hardy for himself

6   Hardy's study at Max Gate

I love 'trippers', (I'm always chaffed about it!) & I love to see them enjoying themselves. Besides, I think one's no *right* to, always, shut a thing up, that others want to see. Though Henry declares 'once a week, for the house, & *four* days a week for the grounds, is *enough*' when he is at home – However, as he won't be, on Monday, he's – laughingly – given me leave to let 'my friends, the trippers', over grounds, & house, & to what he calls 'cavort' (!!) in his absence.

Lady Hoare seems to have visited Max Gate, the house that Hardy designed on the outskirts of Dorchester, early in the relationship, meeting Emma, and the Max Gate cats, but it is not clear from the letters that survive whether she met Hardy at this time. Invitations to visit Max Gate and Stourhead were made, but were apparently frustrated for various reasons. Lady Hoare's notes in her copy of *The Later Years of Thomas Hardy, 1892–1928* indicate that she and her husband attended dramatisations of Hardy's novels in Dorchester, and the last garden party given by Emma in July 1912, the subject of a sad entry in the biography:

> Meanwhile in July he [Hardy] had returned to Max Gate just in time to be at a garden party on July 16 – the last his wife ever gave – which it would have much grieved him afterwards to have missed. The afternoon was sunny and the guests numerous . . . and nobody foresaw the shadow that was so soon to fall on the house.

The shadow was, of course, Emma's death at the close of the year – an event that brought sorrow and regret to Hardy, who, remembering their earlier happiness, reproached himself for not doing more to heal the wounds of the marriage. Something of his emotion is revealed in a letter written to Lady Hoare shortly afterwards. The letter is kept in Lady Hoare's copy of *Under the Greenwood Tree*, and was written from Max Gate on 15 December 1912. Thanking Lady Hoare for her sympathy, and for a wreath, Hardy expressed his regret that he had not taken the opportunity of visiting Stourhead with Emma. 'But, alas, I thought her in the soundest health & that there was plenty of time.'

After Emma's death, Florence Dugdale, who had worked with Hardy, and had been a family friend since her first visit to Max Gate in 1904, moved into the house to restore order to the household. This she certainly did, though at some cost to her own eventual happiness, as can be seen from a letter she wrote to S.C.Cockerell, in 1922:

> Looking back, I seem to see a clear division in my life, for on that day I seemed suddenly to leap from youth into dreary middle age . . . I suppose because I had no responsibility before.

She married Hardy in 1914, an event recorded in the biography in what must be one of the most self-effacing sentences ever written: 'In February of the year following the subject of this memoir married the present writer.' It was this marriage, however, that brought the Hardy association with Stourhead to fullness.

The secret wedding, in Enfield, is the subject of a card written by Hardy to Lady Hoare on 13 February 1914, in which Hardy apologised for not telling her beforehand about the wedding, and introduced Florence as 'a literary woman, but not a blue-stocking at all'. The phrase is a reminder that Hardy did not approve his wife's desire to continue her career as a writer.

Five days later, on the 18th, Lady Hoare made what was for her a memorable visit to Max Gate, in response to Hardy's invitation. It is recorded in a note on the inside cover of Lady Hoare's copy of Hermann Lea's *Thomas Hardy's Wessex*:

> This afternoon, Feb 18th, I motored, from Stourhead, to Stinsford Churchyard, &, thence, walked down to the river path; leading to Bockhampton Bridge; opening scene of that beautiful work *Under the Greenwood Tree* – thence, I motored to Max Gate, where I had the privilege of having tea, with Thomas Hardy & Mrs Hardy – curiously he chanced to have been just re-reading the MS of *Under the Greenwood Tree*, for a new edition, thereof – I was so fortunate as to be shown, by Mrs Hardy, the MS of *The Woodlanders* – Deeply interested in the Great author's *Wessex*, – on which I already had lesser books than this, I asked him re 'the best': he recommended *this*: the author of which, now, resides in Thomas Hardy's own birthplace: see page XIX – on leaving Max Gate I drove to Ling's in the old High-East Street; & purchased this book; in 'souvenir' of one afternoon of rare, (very rare!) interest, & pleasure. (A.H.)

Florence, too, valued the visit highly, perhaps welcoming the acknowledgment it made of her new role, and she wrote, 'I am sure it will always remain with me as one of the most delightful memories of my early married days.' The visit occasioned the gift of a tea-strainer, for which Florence thanked Lady Hoare in a letter of 8 March. There is no indication of any gentle irony in the present, though in other letters Florence speaks of her own inexperience of house-keeping.

Lady Hoare appears to have remembered Hardy's birthday each year, and sent small gifts, which Hardy acknowledged punctiliously. Despite Evelyn Hardy's comment in her book, *Thomas Hardy: a critical biography* (1954), that Hardy did not like presents, he always responded warmly to those from Stourhead – Lady Hoare's gifts, and the game frequently sent by Sir Henry Hoare. In June 1918, for instance, he thanked Lady Hoare for her present of candle-snuffers, and a door-knocker which Florence apparently offered to put on his study door, though, Hardy added, 'I am sure she will scorn to use it, but burst in as unceremoniously as usual.'

In May 1914, Lady Hoare again went to Dorchester, this time visiting Hermann Lea, who lived in Hardy's birthplace at Higher Bockhampton (now, like Stourhead, owned by the National Trust, and occasionally open to visitors). A photograph of the cottage is kept in her copy of *The Dynasts*, together with the note:

> This photo of the birthplace of the great author was given me on the afternoon of May 19, 1914 by Mr Hermann Lea, at present residing there. He most kindly invited me to tea to see this most beautiful spot. Mrs Thomas Hardy kindly acted cicerone. I later, with Mrs Hardy, motored to Max Gate, and was received by the great author. A red-letter day indeed.

We learn from an entry on the end paper of her copy of *Time's Laughing Stocks*, that this was followed by a visit by the whole family to Max Gate:

> On Sat July 23rd (1914) Henry, Harry and I had the privilege of making Hardy's acquaintance; he gave us tea at his residence, Max Gate, near Dorchester. I expressed

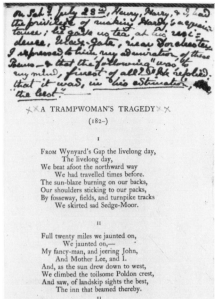

On Sat.ᵈ July 28ᵗʰ, Henry, Harry, & I had
the privilege of making Hardy's acquaintance: he gave us tea, at his residence, Wolsey-Gate, near Dorchester.
I expressed to him my admiration of these Poems — & that the "following" was, to my mind, finest of all? & he replied that it was, in his estimation, "the best."

A TRAMPWOMAN'S TRAGEDY

(182–)

I

FROM Wynyard's Gap the livelong day,
          The livelong day,
We beat afoot the northward way
          We had travelled times before.
The sun-blaze burning on our backs,
Our shoulders sticking to our packs,
By fosseway, fields, and turnpike tracks
          We skirted sad Sedge-Moor.

II

Full twenty miles we jaunted on,
          We jaunted on,—
My fancy-man, and jeering John,
          And Mother Lee, and I.
And, as the sun drew down to west,
We climbed the toilsome Poldon crest,
And saw, of landskip sights the best,
          The inn that beamed thereby.

7 Hardy's birthplace. The cottage at Bockhampton, now a property of the National Trust

8 An annotated page from Lady Hoare's copy of *Time's Laughing Stocks* by Thomas Hardy, first published in 1909

to him an admiration of these poems, and that the following (*The Tramp-woman's Tragedy*) was, to my mind, the finest of all. He replied that it was, in his estimation, 'the best'.

Florence appears to have responded immediately to Lady Hoare's evident sympathy and generosity of spirit, and from the outset her letters to Lady Hoare are open and frank. She assumed the role of correspondent on Hardy's behalf, releasing his time for his more serious writing, and preserving his failing eye-sight, though evidently the letters were often written by her with an interested Hardy at her shoulder. She found a real friend in Lady Hoare, and turned to her for advice and, sometimes, comfort. The many letters by her, carefully preserved by Lady Hoare, give insight into her husband's later years, and reveal her own affectionate care of him. On 7 April 1914, for instance, she writes of Hardy's pleasure in his honorary degree at Cambridge University:

> . . . I am full of joy to see how my husband finds himself in his true environment here. He went off just now in his cap & gown – very, *very* pleased with his adornments, to dine in his college (Magdalene) – & he loves being Dr Hardy. He is really just like a boy – or a nice child. . . .
> I often wonder how many people realise the simplicity of his nature. He told me the other day that he thought he had never grown up.

And on 7 July 1914, concerning an anticipated visit to Stourhead, she wrote,

> My husband is looking forward to his visit so much (&, needless to say, I too). There are really *very* few things in the world that he cares about now & fewer people, so that it is a great joy to me to find him so keen about anything.

The visit was made on the weekend of 11 to 13 July 1914. Kenneth Woodbridge, in his excellent book, *Landscape and Antiquity: Aspects of English Culture at Stourhead 1718 to 1838* (1970), writes of Hardy being a 'frequent visitor to Stourhead in his later life', though there is little evidence of other visits in the correspondence. The difficulty of travel during the war years, and Hardy's age and frailty after the war, made visits to Stourhead unlikely, though their absence was often regretted. On the other hand, the Hoares visited Max Gate as often as possible, and their visits were always happy events.

In her copy of Walter de la Mare's *The Listeners*, Lady Hoare wrote that Hardy had a copy of the poems in his pocket when he visited Stourhead, and that he warmly recommended the title poem to her. On this visit, too, in response to her praise of his novels, he said, 'You were very kind about them – I wish to thank you – for you know, really, they are very bad.' Lady Hoare followed this entry in her notes in *The Later Years* with two exclamation marks. The highlight of the visit seems to have been a visit to Stourton Tower in the motorcar with Sir Henry and Harry, the Hoare's only son. This is frequently referred to in later letters, when events made the memory of this happy weekend particularly poignant.

It is clear from other letters that Florence found Hardy's preoccupation with Emma's sudden death, his grief at his neglect of her, and his visits to the old haunts and places associated with the happier, early years of his courtship and first marriage, distressing. Particularly so was the publication of *Satires of Circumstance* in October 1914, which contained many poems written after Emma's death. On 6 December 1914, Florence wrote to Lady Hoare,

> . . . I must confess to you – & I would confess this to no one else – the book pains me horribly, & yet I read it with a terrible fascination. It seems to me that I am an utter failure if my husband can publish such a *sad sad* book. He tells me that he has written *no* despondent poem for the last eighteen months, & yet I cannot get rid of the feeling

9 Stourton Tower. The Hoares drove Hardy here, during his weekend visit to Stourhead in July, 1914

10 and 11 Sir Henry and Lady Hoare, photographed at about the time of Hardy's visit to Stourhead

that the man who wrote some of those poems is utterly weary of life – & cares for nothing in this world. If I had been a different sort of woman, & better fitted to be his wife – would he, I wonder, have published that volume?

Lady Hoare's reply to this moving letter is unfortunately not preserved, but it seems to have given considerable support and comfort, for Florence wrote in her next letter, on 9 December 1914,

Your letter . . . put things straight in my mind . . . Oddly enough, as if to show me how right & just your letter was, he has been particularly bright & cheerful the last day or so. And of course I do know he has a tender protective affection for me – as a father for a child – as he has always had – a feeling quite apart from passion. And I feel towards him, sometimes, as a mother towards a child with whom things have somehow gone wrong – a child who needs comforting – to be treated gently & with all the love possible.

Your letter was – I could almost say inspired, & I shall always feel most grateful for it.

Your promised visit sheds a sort of sunshine over all the days here. He is looking forward to it ever so much. I suggested – rather to tease him than of serious intent – that we should invite some friends to lunch to meet you. His face fell. 'O, that won't be the same thing at all', he said dolefully.

12 *Florence Hardy* (*née Dugdale*) by William Strang, RA, 1910. Pencil drawing, 25.4 by 38 cm (Dorset County Museum)

That Florence found it hard to reconcile herself with her husband's continuing pre-occupation with the past is revealed by a letter written two years later, on 5 September 1916, concerning a visit to Cornwall:

> My husband keeps well & on Thursday we propose going for a brief four days holiday – to revisit his old haunts in Cornwall. I hope that it will not prove a very depressing visit for him. He is going to look up some Giffords too – cousins of the late Mrs T.H – people whom he has never met. As they were not even friendly with her I do rather wish he would not do this. However not for worlds would I suggest that he should not do so. I wish I could be broader-minded & look more philosophically upon life – as I know you do. I feel so mean & petty but I make strenuous efforts to hide it, & am, I hope & believe, successful. One has to go through a kind of mental hoodwinking & blind one's own self to the past, & pretend that things were not as they were, but utterly different.

Domestic problems also occupied her attention in the early years of the marriage, and though she was able to recommend at least one domestic servant to Lady Hoare, the letters show the difficulty she herself had in finding suitable staff for Max Gate. One house parlour-maid, who had been retained out of sympathy for her ill-health,

> after giving a lot of trouble, & stealing some nice things, including a new gold-mounted stylo pen that had been given to my husband, said she would leave as she wanted a holiday, & she departed with her booty. That was a case of misplaced kindness, I'm sure.

The miscreant's successor, a girl who had become deaf as a child after the drums of her ears were destroyed by typhoid, soon gave up work altogether: 'She seems to think she has some kind of claim on us', wrote Florence indignantly.

The events of the next few years, however, brought a new dimension of sorrow. Lady Hoare's son enlisted in the first days of the war in 1914. Hardy wrote his *Song of the Soldiers* as a direct result of his enlistment, as Florence indicates in a letter of 10 September 1914:

> (My husband) asks me to tell you that he scribbled it hastily upon his return from church on Sunday last (where we had an *awful* sermon from a drivelling curate). Indeed he wrote the main part of it while we were at dinner. Bad for his digestion, doubtless. We hope your son is well. It was such as him that my husband had in mind when he wrote 'the faith and fire within us'.

The poem appeared in *The Times*, and Florence commented, 'He had, as always has, a concrete example in his mind when he wrote it.' She sent a specially written copy of this poem to Stourhead as a Christmas card, on which is written, 'Inspired by Harry', with a note added in pencil by Lady Hoare, 'and others like him'.

Harry, (Henry Colt Arthur Hoare; 1888–1917), served as a lieutenant in the 1st Dorset Queen's Own Yeomanry. He was invalided home from the Dardanelles in 1916, but returned to the Middle East to see further action in Palestine. He died in hospital in Alexandria in December 1917 from wounds received at Mughair Ridge a month earlier. It was a tragic blow to Sir Henry and Lady Hoare, doubly so as he was their only child, and, unmarried, left no heir to inherit the estate.

The friendship with the Hardys may have been strengthened by mutual sympathy and sorrow occasioned by this loss. Hardy himself had lost a much valued relation, Lt Frank George, killed at Gallipoli in 1915. Though Hardy had no children, he seems

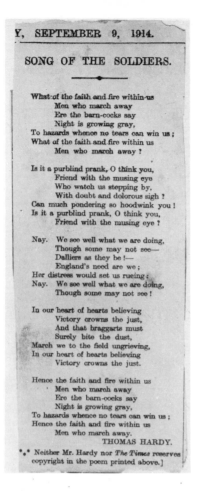

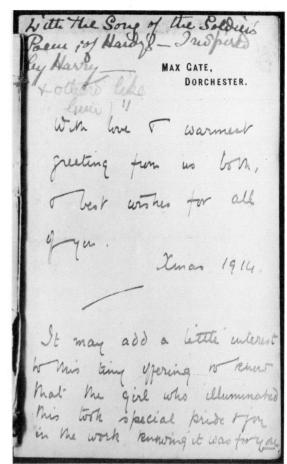

to have felt deeply for Sir Henry and Lady Hoare during their years of anxiety and loss. His own desire for a child has been recorded elsewhere, but it is mentioned in the Stourhead correspondence in a letter from Florence, written towards the end of the war, on 22 April 1918. She refers in the letter to Lady Hoare's excellent criticism of Hardy's latest volume of poems, *Moments of Vision*, in which many of his war poems appeared, and mentions, obliquely, the deaths of Frank George and Henry Hoare. The letter continues by discussing the problems that would arise if Florence's sister, who was expecting a child, came to stay at Max Gate after the birth of the child, or if the child arrived prematurely if she stayed with them before the birth:

> . . . there would be a fine fuss & trouble for my poor husband. He is genuinely afraid of babies – & why, after all, should he be bothered with all this fuss for another man's wife & child.
>
> . . . Babies seem to choose to come where there is little room for them, & to carefully avoid going where their presence would be most eagerly welcomed. A man who worked for my husband's father was told by his parson that 'God sent babies, but He also sent bread'. 'Aye' replied the man, 'But he sends the babies to one house & the bread to another.'
>
> How eagerly a baby would have been welcomed in *this* house – Max Gate – years ago!

One cannot imagine this comment being made without the tragic circumstances which preceded it, and without an implicit trust in Lady Hoare's friendship.

This trust extended to trust in her sympathetic literary judgements, and on many occasions Hardy sent early drafts of poems to her for comment, among them an interesting version of *The Dead and the Living One*, which varies considerably from the

14 *Lady Hoare playing to troops from Mere Hospital in the Music Room at Stourhead* by St George Hare, 1918. Pen and wash 27 by 20 cm (National Trust, Stourhead, Wiltshire)

poem as published in its final form (Lady Hoare's copy of the early version can be found at Trowbridge). Lady Hoare was certainly in sympathy with Hardy's philosophical attitudes. In her copy of Florence's biography, opposite the war poem, *England at Bay*, she wrote that it was not written out of despair. 'I don't find "despair" in Hardy, anywhere – melancholy only.'

Without doubt the war deepened Hardy's melancholy, and Florence, too, caught the mood in some of her later letters. After Hardy had made a tiring journey to London in 1920, she wrote:

> It was an effort for him rather, & I am not sure that he will be wise to go to London again. How sad life seems at times – indeed it is always sad, only sometimes we do not perceive the sadness.

Lady Hoare's enthusiasm for Hardy's work continued unabated. She read and re-read the novels and poems, looking forward eagerly to the new volumes of poems as they appeared, and reading them appreciatively. She read the major works of criticism, and, at least on one occasion, in 1922, translated an article about Hardy's poetry from the *Echo de Paris* to send to him. She sent it with a pilgrim's bottle for a mummers' play, a reminder of Hardy's continuing interest in, and active support of, amateur drama in Dorchester in his later years.

If she gave Florence comfort in the early years of the marriage, she evidently gave consolation after Hardy's death. There is no evidence of meetings, but her letters were a continual support. Kenneth Woodbridge is right to say that 'perhaps the most interesting cultural association (at Stourhead, in Sir Henry's lifetime) was with Thomas Hardy, whose sense of antiquity found many affinities at Stourhead, and who was, perhaps, the last great exponent of landscape in English literature.' But the real value of the association was in the personal friendships that endured over two decades. The letters, for all their literary interest, are finally most moving as human documents, recording intimate details in the lives of the writers. At the end of the letter of 7 September 1931, mentioned at the beginning of this article, Florence wrote, 'I am glad you liked the statue – I thought, really, there were some beautiful things in [Barrie's] speech.' Then, moving from the public event to the private life, she added,

> In the pocket of the last coat T.H. wore I found, after his death, just an old knife, an unfinished poem, & a piece of string.

15   The Library at Stourhead, with Hardy's signed photograph on the desk on the foreground

Acknowledgments
I should like to express my thanks to Mr Bateman and his staff at Stourhead, to Mr Dudley Dodd, Mr Rennie Hoare, Lloyds Bank, Trust Division, Mr Maurice Rathbone, Wiltshire County Archivist and the trustees of the Thomas Hardy Memorial Collection at the Dorset County Museum. A particular debt of gratitude is due to Mr Frederick Grice, who helped with the research.

1 The East Front,
Stourhead. Figs 1, 2 and 6
are from a set of
photographs taken on 16
April 1902, the day of the
fire

2 The Entrance Hall,
Stourhead, 1902

Rebuilding Stourhead 1902-1906

DUDLEY DODD

DISASTROUS FIRE

STOURHEAD MANSION ABLAZE

CENTRE OF THE HOUSE GUTTED

MANY VALUABLE PAINTINGS DESTROYED[1]

It would be tempting to dismiss these headlines as over-sensational were it not for the photographs of Stourhead taken on 16 April 1902, the day of the fire (Figs 1, 2 and 6). In this melancholy record smoulder the ruins of the great house, designed by Colen Campbell about 1718 for the successful London banker, Henry Hoare I.[2]

When Horace Walpole visited Stourhead in 1762[3] he found the rooms 'in general too low', but 'richly furnished'; the list of paintings reveals the quality of the collection formed by Henry Hoare II, aptly named Henry 'the Magnificent'. His heir, Sir Richard Colt Hoare, 2nd Bart, was a scholar and connoisseur. Soon after returning from Europe in 1791, he built the Library and Picture Gallery which flank the main facade and commissioned new furniture for the house from Thomas Chippendale the younger.[4] But when he died in 1838 the house must have been distinctly old-fashioned and a contemporary inventory[5] describes carpets and curtains worn thin and upholstery and case covers in threadbare condition. Sir Henry Hoare, 3rd Bart, busied himself building the entrance portico to Campbell's original design and it was not until 1857 that Sir Henry Ainslie Hoare, 5th Bart, began any renovations. Sadly, his enthusiasm was short-lived and he neglected Stourhead for the next four decades, eventually plundering the house to pay his debts. It was fortunate that his cousin, Sir Henry Hoare, 6th Bart, had the energy and resources to rescue the property. Within a year of inheriting he left his home, Wavendon, in Buckinghamshire and moved to Stourhead with his wife, Alda Weston, and their only son, Henry. He set out to restore the house, installing new services, redecorating all the rooms and rearranging the contents, to include the furniture from Wavendon. This task was completed in 1897[6] and all the main rooms were then photographed (Figs 13-15).

Five years later Sir Henry stood on the south lawn looking at the glowing embers of the house. 'He seemed to take the matter somewhat coolly, if outward appearances count for anything' according to *The Western Gazette*, 'he walked up and down the lawn smoking cigarettes. But conversation with him revealed intense sorrow at what was taking place around him.'[7] The fire began in a chimney flue and spread to the ceiling void. The housemaids gave the alarm after breakfast when they discovered the bedrooms filled with smoke. Soon the upper floors were ablaze and the flames broke through the roof. Sir Henry and Lady Hoare had both gone away for the day but the staff acted sensibly; they began rescuing the contents of the *piano nobile* and, with help from the estate workers, man-handled the pictures and furniture to safety through the windows. The *Gazette* continues the story,

> While all this was being accomplished by the household, fire-engines, hand-pumps, and hose-carts were arriving from all parts. Frome sent their powerful steamer, under Captain Rawlings, Mere a manual in charge of Captain Mallet, while later arrived appliances from Colonel Browne, of Zeals House, Lord Stalbridge, of Motcombe, and

the Hon. Percy Wyndham, of 'Clouds', East Knoyle. Unfortunately, however, there was little water for their use. The nearest was the lake well over a quarter of a mile away. The Frome steamer was stationed on the bank, and the necessary piping quickly joined up, and for several hours a steady pressure was maintained. But it was no use. The flames had got hold too firmly. Every moment the extent of the fire became greater, and scarcely had the last piece of furniture been moved when the roof fell in. A renewed onset of the flames and the ceilings fell through also, tongues of fire leaped out all round, and soon the central block became a glowing furnace.

The fight continued well into the afternoon when flames began to travel along the roof of the corridor to the Library. But fortunately this new outbreak was controlled.

The extent of the damage was daunting and of all the splendid interiors, only the Library and the Picture Gallery survived. The contents of the upper floors perished, including items from Wavendon and the furniture acquired by Sir Richard Colt Hoare in 1816, 'pretium ultra £2,000',[8] presumably supplied by Thomas Chippendale the younger. Some sixty paintings were destroyed in the Inner Hall although they were, according to Sir Richard himself, 'of the second class'.[9] More serious was the loss of big paintings from the set of seven in the Large Dining Room (Colour plate XI);[10] *The Rape of Helen*, after Guido Reni and *The Death of Dido*, after Guercino, which flanked the chimney-piece and *The Judgement of Midas*, by Sebastien Bourdon on the wall opposite.[11] These were an integral part of the decoration of the room created by Henry 'the Magnificent' in 1744–46 and thereafter acclaimed as the most splendid in the house. It was designed by Henry Flitcroft[12] with a magnificent chimney-piece carved by Sefferin Alken.[13] The accounts include payments to distinguished local craftsmen, such as Francis Cartwright of Blandford[14] and Francis Price, Surveyor of Salisbury Cathedral.[15]

If ever Sir Henry hesitated over the reconstruction of the house, he did not trouble to record his doubts. The property was fully insured and building materials and labour

3 *Sir Aston Webb* by S. J. Solomon, *c* 1906. Canvas, 88.7 by 71.2 cm (National Portrait Gallery)

4   Sir Henry and Lady Hoare with their son Henry and 'Sweep' on 4 October 1912

were relatively cheap. Moreover the country-house tradition still flourished, thanks to the excellent railway service, and rekindled enthusiasm for country pursuits, in particular for shooting parties. Two architects are associated with the reconstruction, Sir Aston Webb and Edward Doran Webb. The coincidence of the surname causes confusion, although the two men were neither related, nor business associates. Sir Aston Webb (1849–1930)[16] had a thriving practice in London and specialised in the great public buildings to which Edwardians were addicted. With Edward Ingress Bell, he designed the Cromwell Road front of the Victoria and Albert Museum (1899–1909) and the University of Birmingham (1900–1909) at Edgbaston. He also devised the scheme for the Mall (1901), with Admiralty Arch (1911) and the new east front of Buckingham Palace (1913).

By contrast little is known at present about Doran Webb, who had an office in Salisbury from about 1889. Thomas Stevens, the Hoare's solicitor, once referred to him as 'the great master of Ecclesiastical Architecture'[17] and *The Buildings of England* mentions him as the architect of several local churches[18] and Blackfriars (1921–29),[19] the Dominican priory at Oxford. Long before the fire he was on friendly terms with the Hoares and a frequent visitor to Stourhead. In 1897 he designed the terrace at the

Ground plan marked with amendments

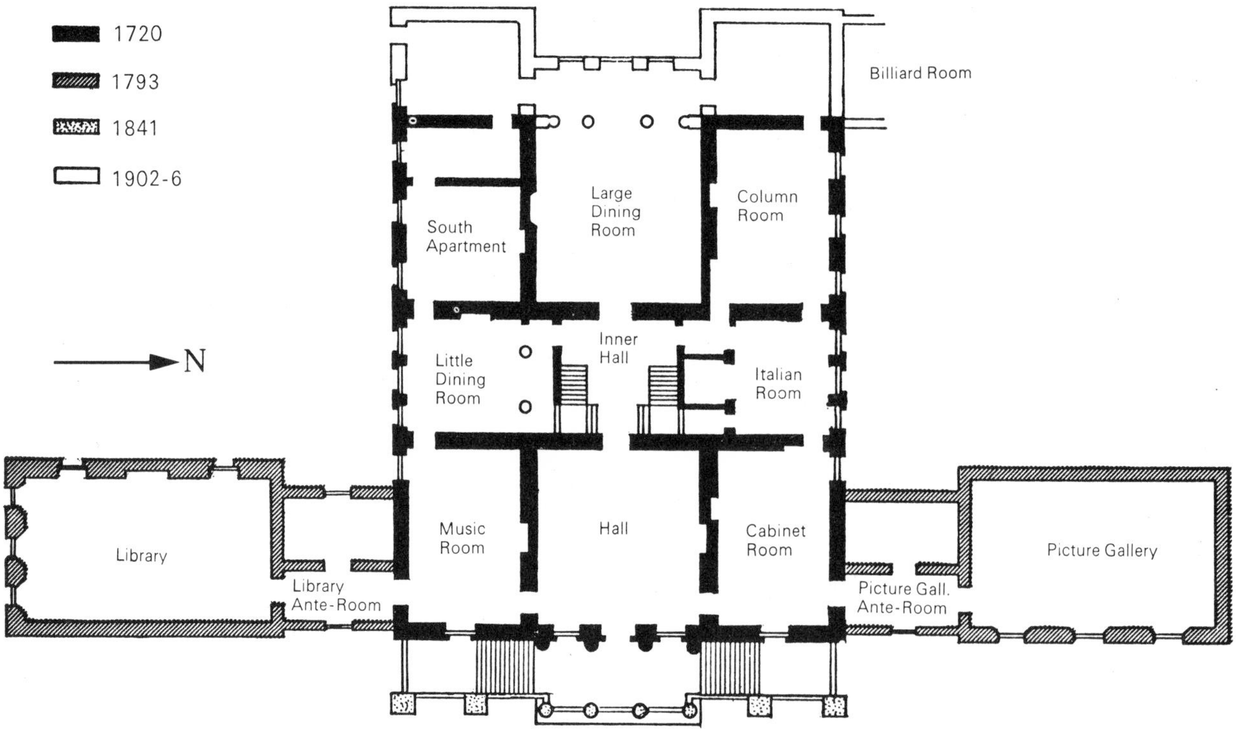

5 Ground plan of Stourhead

south-west corner of the house and his letters to Sir Henry show how the friendship grew. The shortcomings of a local craftsman were the subject of much lighthearted banter on his part, 'why did not you bury the plumber in one of the holes of his own making . . .' he wrote 'or . . . quarter him on the stone shield in place of the eagle?'.[20]

The Stourhead guidebook of 1907 explains that 'Sir Henry Hoare commenced the work of restoration immediately, Mr Doran Webb, of Salisbury, and afterwards, Sir Aston Webb, Bart, being the architects'. More informative is the footnote written by Lady Hoare in the Library copy, 'Mr Doran Webb, early, proving unequal, he was replaced, on dismissal, by Sir Aston Webb.'[21] It is not the purpose here to chronicle how bitterness and animosity supplanted friendship between the parties, but to assess the contribution of the architects, from evidence in the Stourhead Annals and the surviving drawings[22] and letters.

Reconstruction began on 16 June 1902 and, from the outset, local craftsmen and materials were used. Sir Henry describes how 'the stone employed in the building all came from the Doulting Quarries, being hauled by my own Traction Engine. The bricks from Bourton and Gillingham, and the lime from the White Sheet Quarry.'[23] The builder was Charles Trask and Sons of Norton-sub-Hamdon.

Of the original house, three outside walls survived in reasonable condition but the west front (Fig 6) was badly damaged, and had to be demolished. In its place Doran Webb ventured a new design with two projecting wings and a recessed centre, the upper part set further back behind a screen of columns with a pediment (Fig 7). This feature is the weakest element of the façade; diminutive in scale and perched above the *piano nobile* it contrasts with the great entrance portico, a faint echo of true Palladian architecture. Moreover the screen darkens the bedrooms behind and shelters a chilly, cramped balcony. The wings become two extra bays on the side elevations where

Campbell symmetrical design[24] was already disfigured by the Library on the south and by the Picture Gallery and some smaller accretions on the north. Above the service wing in the North Court Doran Webb built a new Billiard Room, a larger edition of the Justice Room which was there before the fire. He also added a balustrade to the roofs of the Library and Picture Gallery.

At first the work progressed swiftly and by December 1902 Doran Webb wrote with élan,

> 'we have managed to get most of the structural work done at an exceedingly moderate cost, the actual amount spent from April last up to 11th December was £3,300 ... I hope we shall get the building roofed in and the attic floor completed for £10,000. I believe the south wing will be ready for occupation by Christmas 1903.'[25]

Sir Henry replanned the first floor, making corridors (where previously the only access to the rooms was the communicating doors) and forming two more bedrooms on the west side. To achieve this Doran Webb had to lower the ceiling in the Large Dining Room below, destroying for ever its noble proportions. Further 'improvements' were made to the *piano nobile*. There were impressive vistas from the Picture Gallery to the Library and from the front door to the Large Dining Room. Sir Henry took the opportunity to enhance the latter and open a new enfilade from the Italian Room to the Little Dining Room by rearranging the Inner Hall (Fig 5).[26] In place of the original single staircase Doran Webb put twin flights and galleries reminiscent of the great hall at Coleshill (*c*1650) in Berkshire, although the confined space makes it a 'cottage' version with steep and narrow steps. By extending the house westwards Doran Webb was able to squeeze a second staircase in the south-west corner, lengthen the Large Dining Room and make an imposing approach (subsequently modified) to the new Billiard Room beyond. He also rearranged the Cabinet Room introducing a window in the north wall, a door through to the Italian Room and a new chimney-piece. When it came to reinstating the decoration Sir Henry wanted accurate replicas. He described with pride how Signor Agostini of Bristol copied the plasterwork for the Entrance Hall, Little Dining Room, Column Room and Italian Room from the old photographs and fragments of the original work gathered after the fire. But in the Italian Room he wisely decided not to reproduce the painted decoration described by Horace Walpole as 'pretty taste'. All the rooms in the original house lost their chimney-pieces apart from the Music Room, Little Dining Room and South Apartment. A replica chimney-piece was made for the Entrance Hall but those in the Column Room and Italian Room came from Wavendon in 1912-13. At the same time the great chimney-piece was moved from the Library to the Large Dining Room. The origin of the chimney-piece in the Cabinet Room has not yet been discovered. Sir Henry replaced the stone floor in the two halls with marble and put teak parquet in the Large Dining Room, Column Room and Italian Room. Among other 'straight' Edwardian features surviving today are the fire-places lined with red glazed bricks and fitted with shiny copper hoods and the unusual, but almost invisible, leaded skylight on the new Billiard Room (Fig 11). Of course Sir Henry allowed himself modern comforts, such as electric light and bells, radiators and, understandably, fire hydrants, served by a 150,000 gallon reservoir, commissioned in 1903 'to supply the house and insure protection from fire'.[27]

At Christmas 1903 Doran Webb admitted spending £4,650 above his previous estimate but still the house was uninhabitable. Seven months later the Hoares were able

6 The West Front,
Stourhead, 1902

7 The West Front,
Stourhead, today

to move into the south-west corner where to their dismay they discovered 'the noise in the house was intolerable, voices being heard distinctly from floor to floor'.[28] Doran Webb made 'countless futile attempts' at sound-proofing but in September Sir Henry, losing patience, brought in an expert. Sir Aston Webb agreed to visit Stourhead (at a fee of 20 guineas) to advise specifically 'as to how best prevent sound in a large home'.[29] Doran Webb did not refer to the visit; his silence is understandable for Sir Aston pronounced the only cure as 'double joists' throughout. With stoic forbearance Sir Henry wrote, 'this necessitated pulling out the whole of the ceilings of the south wing basement, reception and bedroom floors also the Music Room, Italian Room and north wing bedroom floors, which has done by degrees, involving an enormous amount of extra expense and discomfort.'[30] Furthermore the lawyers advised against suing Doran Webb for negligence. At about this time Sir Henry appointed Wooldridge as the main contractor at the house, after dismissing Trask for receiving illicit commissions.

That winter, young Henry Hoare was 'very ill with his heart'[31] and in early 1905 Sir Henry took him to Egypt to convalesce. Lady Hoare remained at Stourhead watching the work with growing anxiety. The ceilings in the Entrance Hall and the Large Dining Room began to sag alarmingly and on 17 March the Pantry chimney caught fire. Fortunately it was soon put out but the incident sparked a crisis between Lady Hoare and

8 *Alda Weston, Lady Hoare* by St George Hare, 1909. Canvas, 150 by 92 cm (National Trust, Stourhead, Wiltshire)

9 The Large Dining Room, Stourhead

Doran Webb, which is chronicled in her daily letters to Thomas Stevens, the family solicitor. At first he merely commiserated and offered tentative explanations 'I suppose the span of the ceiling of the big Dining Room was too wide for the weight of the ceiling itself'.[32] But Lady Hoare was in high dudgeon and she attributed the Pantry fire to the design of the flue which prevented the chimney from being swept. Her next meeting with Doran Webb was a painful experience; 'I was *not* out of temper but firm' she wrote, but the interview lasted exactly ten minutes and he left 'without Adieu'.[33] Stevens worked to keep the peace. He met Doran Webb in London and reported that the architect had answered 'the file of indictment and promised to visit Stourhead once a fortnight'.[34] Lady Hoare was not appeased, she itemised new defects in the work and rounded on poor Stevens for protecting the culprit. Soon afterwards Mrs Doran Webb sent a long, very injudicious letter to Lady Hoare, 'Mr Webb is seriously ill from the effects', she wrote 'and if he is to continue his work at Stourhead it can only be done by your standing aside; otherwise I must bring all the influence I can to bear on him to throw up the whole thing and at once.'[35] This untimely plea hastened the dénouement and within a few days his resignation was tendered and promptly accepted. Ruefully he wrote 'the only details not yet designed are the doors and architraves to the Large Dining Room and the Doors under the Staircase to the Basement' with a touch of melodrama in the postscript 'I shall leave for France by the last train from here on Friday.'[36]

It was doubtless Sir Aston Webb's successful intervention at Stourhead in 1904, that prompted Stevens to approach him as successor to Doran Webb. At first Sir Aston

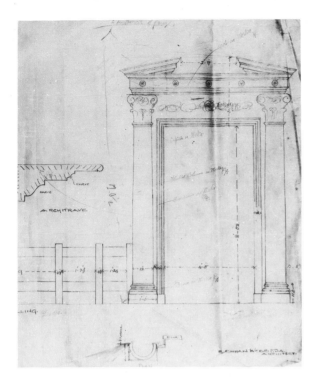

10 Drawing for the 'Door to Inner Hall from Dining Room' by E. Doran Webb, annotated by Sir Aston Webb and dated 17 July 1905. Pen and ink, 45.5 by 77 cm (National Trust, Stourhead, Wiltshire)

11 *Above right* Drawing for a 'Detail of Glazing to Ends of Billiard Room Skylight', by Sir Aston Webb, dated 16 October 1905. Pen and wash, 52.5 by 42.5 cm (National Trust, Stourhead, Wiltshire)

declined, 'the distance is so great that I am afraid I could not give the necessary personal attention to the completion of Stourhead House'.[37] A renewed plea brought his recommendation of a reputable local architect and almost as an afterthought this suggestion, 'I have a son helping me here but I have hesitated mentioning him'.[38] This appointment was clinched when Sir Henry returned from Egypt in May. Henceforth work at Stourhead was directed from Sir Aston Webb's office in London, and supervised on site by his experienced clerk of works. Maurice Webb visited the house frequently.

Their main task was to stabilise the structure and then to complete the restoration. For architects accustomed to large buildings, sagging ceilings were a straightforward engineering problem. But the massive steel girders installed are an ugly reminder of the inadequacy of Doran Webb's work. For the west front, Sir Aston Webb designed a flight of steps crossing the basement court in a graceful curve (safely supported by girders). He also added the balustrade to the portico above; its undulating profile lends a baroque smirk to the somewhat lifeless classical mask. Inside, mahogany doors were ordered from London and Signor Agostini made good the damaged ceilings and completed the plasterwork in the Column Room and Italian Room. The decorations in the Large Dining Room, potentially the grandest room in the house, had still to be decided. Of course, Doran Webb had altered the proportions by lowering the ceiling and extending it westwards, marking the line of the old hall with a screen of stone columns. He had also designed the new plasterwork ceiling with a stiff geometric rib-pattern – a poor substitute for the rich eighteenth-century coved ceiling. Sir Aston Webb paused before completing the room and wrote

> I understand that Mr Doran Webb suggested pilasters on the walls and tapestry between but as I believe you have some large pictures to go in this room, I think it would be better to omit the pilasters which would probably be in the way and treat the walls in some other way. I think it was decided to paint the whole of it white and if this is done pilasters will not, I think be necessary.[39]

In the end he also redesigned the entrance (Fig 10) adding swags when Sir Henry criticised the ornament as meagre.

By summer 1906 the house was complete and Sir Henry declared himself well satisfied, 'Sir Aston Webb and his Son Mr Maurice Webb were most efficient, and carried out everything entrusted to them to our entire satisfaction.'[40] The work cost £43,330 and the balance of the insurance money was earmarked 'to provide for the anticipated re-painting and re-decoration a few years hence, of the Mansion and offices.'[41]

In view of this achievement, it seems churlish to accuse Sir Henry of under-estimating the problems of the reconstruction; but if his first choice of architect proved a false economy, so too did his reliance on provincial craftsmen. Today the sensitive visitor will notice the variable quality in ornamental features, such as the door architraves

(Fig 12) and chimney-piece in the Entrance Hall; in photographs the carving appears a convincing replica of the original but on close inspection the detail looks dead.

It is tantalising that there are apparently no photographs of the rooms in 1906, making it hard to assess how far the Hoares were influenced by new fashions in furnishings. They did not repeat the bold patterned floral wallpapers, so conspicuous in the 1890s photographs; instead they had the main rooms painted throughout, though more perhaps to allow the plaster to dry thoroughly than in response to the progress of taste from Morris's designs. Correspondence suggests that the Hoares were conservative in these matters. Early on Doran Webb had scorned their request for roller blinds as belonging 'to the same period as the wax flowers, antemacassars, woolwork, horse-hair

14 The Music Room,
Stourhead, c 1898

15 The Library,
Stourhead, c 1898

Plate XI *The Large Dining Room, Stourhead* by J. C. Buckler, 1824. Watercolour, 25.6 by 36.8 cm (Collection: Mr Paul Mellon)

chairs, gilded abominations of all sorts that came in with the late Prince Consort. Having been fortunate enough to get the things burnt I cannot conceive anyone going out of their way to put the things back.'[42] Most of these taboo items feature in the early photographs of Stourhead when the rooms were crowded with furniture of all periods, presided over by massive palms and potted ferns (Figs 13, 14 and 15). Because most of the furniture survived, Lady Hoare would have had no difficulty in refilling the main rooms, crowding china and pot plants on every available surface in the late nineteenth-century tradition. But she also found conspicuous places for contemporary paintings by her favourite artist, St George Hare.

His portraits help evoke the Edwardian era at Stourhead, but if visitors today feel a twinge of nostalgia, few perhaps would wish to return to those days. Moreover, in many instances it has now been possible to put the pictures and Chippendale furniture in rooms for which they were acquired by Sir Richard Colt Hoare. Sir Henry and Lady Hoare recreated the appropriate setting for the collection but this was only the beginning of their achievement. For the next forty years they worked to maintain the estate through two world wars and they continued to make significant improvements to almost every part of it. When Sir Henry bequeathed the property to the National Trust in 1946, we all became the beneficiaries of their single-minded determination to preserve and to share a unique inheritance.

Notes

1 *Western Gazette*, 18 April 1902, p 2.

2 Kenneth Woodbridge, *Landscape and Antiquity* (Oxford, 1970), p 19. The detailed study of Stourhead, 1718-1838.

3 Horace Walpole, 'Journals of Visits to Country Seats', XXVI (1762), ed P. Toynbee, *The Walpole Society*, XVI (1927-28), pp 41-44.

4 See John Kenworthy-Browne, 'Notes on the Furniture by Thomas Chippendale the Younger at Stourhead', *The National Trust Year Book* (1975/76), pp 93-102.

5 Wiltshire Record Office, WRO 383/3/16. I am indebted to the staff of the Record Office for information gained from the Stourhead papers.

6 *Stourhead Annals* II, July 1896 to July 1897. The Annals comprise three bound manuscript volumes, kept at Stourhead, which record building, planting, game, etc. on the estate, 1792-1947.

7 *Western Gazette*, *op cit*.

8 *Stourhead Annals* I, January 1816-17.

9 Sir Richard Colt Hoare, *History of Modern Wiltshire; The Hundred of Mere* (London, 1822), p 81.

10 In this article the rooms are identified by the names used by Sir Henry Hoare. Today the Large Dining Room is known as the Saloon, as it was in the eighteenth and early nineteenth century.

11 *Stourhead Mansion*, *Guidebook* (Wincanton, 1894), p 9.

12 I am indebted to Miss Juliet Allan for this information.

13 C. Hoare & Co., 37 Fleet Street, London, Henry Hoare II, Ledger of Personal Accounts, 1734 to 1749, 'Wilberry' Ledger. Payment on 14 May 1745 to 'Sefferin Alken for ye Saloon Chimney etc. in full of all Demands. £187.10.4.'

14 Ibid, Payment on 22 December 1744 to 'Fra^s Cartwright on Acco^t of ye Saloon £50'.

15 WRO, 383/2/6 Henry Hoare II, Ledger of Personal Accounts 1749 to 1770. Payment on 29 November 1752 to 'Mr. Price of Sarum D^o on Saloon Acco^t given in full £10.10.0'.

16 H. Buckeley Creswell (ed Alastair Service), 'Sir Aston Webb and his Office', *Edwardian Architecture and its Origins* (London 1975), pp 328-37.

17 WRO, 383/12/131, Thomas Stevens to Alda Hoare, 27 March 1905.

18 John Newman and Sir Nikolaus Pevsner, *Dorset* (London, 1972), p 364. In Shaftesbury, the lower chancel of Holy Trinity Church, 1908. Sir Nikolaus Pevsner, *Wiltshire* (revised by Bridget Cherry, London, 1975), pp 356 and 508. In Swindon, Holy Rood Church, 1905, and in Newtown, the Church, 1911.

19 Jennifer Sherwood and Sir Nikolaus Pevsner, *Oxfordshire* (London, 1974), p 314.

20 WRO, 383/12/131. E. Doran Webb to Henry Hoare, 4 August 1897.

21 George Sweetman, *Guide to Stourhead*, *Wilts* (Wincanton, 1907), p 36.

22 An incomplete set of working drawings for the house *c* 1902-1906 by Doran Webb and Sir Aston Webb are kept at Stourhead.

23 *Stourhead Annals* II, July 1901 to July 1902.

24 Colen Campbell, *Vitruvius Britannicus*, III (1725), pl 43.

25 WRO, 383/12/131. E.D.W. to T.S. 23 December 1902.

26 I am indebted to Mr H. P. R. Hoare for information about Sir Henry's motives for altering the layout of the house.

27 *Stourhead Annals* II, July 1903 to July 1904.

28 *Stourhead Annals* II, July 1904 to July 1905.

29 WRO, 383/12/131. Aston Webb to A.H., 16 September 1904.

30 *Stourhead Annals* II, July 1904 to July 1905.

31 *Stourhead Annals* II, July 1904 to July 1905.

32 WRO, 383/12/131, T.S. to A.H., 30 March 1905.

33 WRO, 383/12/131, undated memorandum from A.H. includes a description of this meeting on 28 March 1905.

34 WRO, 383/12/131, T.S. to A.H., 31 March 1905.

35 WRO, 383/12/131, Mrs Doran Webb to A.H., 4 April 1905.

36 WRO, 383/12/131, E.D.W. to T.S., 23 April 1905.

37 WRO, 383/12/131, A.W. to T.S., 13 April 1905.

38 WRO, 383/12/131, A.W. to T.S., 25 April 1905.

39 WRO, 383/12/131, A.W. to H.H., 4 October 1905.

40 *Stourhead Annals* II, July 1905 to July 1906.

41 *Stourhead Annals* II, July 1906 to July 1907. 'An examination of the accounts relating to the expenditure on the Mansion and its contents, showed, that of the £47,200 paid by the Insurance Company, there had been spent:

In rebuilding the Mansion, including the installation of the Electric lighting, Plant and fittings £35,000

For sundry expenses connected with the episode of the fire, salvage of furniture, Insurance of building and furniture during the reconstruction, and miscellaneous matters £1,090

For water wheel, pumps, reservoir, pipes etc. for completing the scheme for a water supply to Mansion, Stables and Gardens, with extensions to the Village and to the farms in the neighbourhood of Stourhead £3,880

For repairing and renovating Pictures and Furniture, damaged by the fire, the purchase of Pictures and furniture, carpets, curtains, linen, and other household effects £3,360

£43,330'

42 WRO, 383/12/131, E.D.W. to H.H., 22 February 1904.

Hubert le Sueur's Portraits of King Charles I in Bronze, at Stourhead, Ickworth and elsewhere

CHARLES AVERY

1 *Hubert Le Sueur* by Claude Warin, bronze portrait medallion, initialled and dated 1635 (British Museum)

The importance of King Charles I as a patron of the arts, as a collector and as a connoisseur cannot be overestimated. He has received wide acclaim for his successful patronage of painting with Rubens and Van Dyck, but less notice has been taken of his attempt to raise the level of sculpture in England by recruiting artists of merit from abroad.[1] He had been conscious of sculpture from an early age, as decoration for palace and garden, and for the promotion of what today is called a 'public image'.

After the premature death of his elder brother, Henry, Prince of Wales, he inherited an entire collection of bronze statuettes by Giambologna, which had been sent as a diplomatic gift by the Medici Grand-Duke in 1611.[2] When he went to Spain in 1623 in connection with a Spanish marriage, he was given the only marble statue by Giambologna ever to have left Italy, the *Samson and a Philistine*, now in the Victoria and Albert Museum.[3] Subsequently, he purchased from the Gonzaga Dukes of Mantua not only their Italian Renaissance paintings, including Mantegna's series of *Triumphs of Julius Caesar* (Hampton Court), but also a huge collection of Graeco-Roman statuary at a cost of £10,000.[4] Henry Peacham summed up Charles's achievement in his manual of polite behaviour, *The Compleat Gentleman*, published in 1634, as follows: 'ever since his coming to the Crowne, (he) hath amply testified a Royall liking of ancient statues, by causing a whole army of old forraine Emperours, Captaines, and Senators all at once to land on his coasts, to come and doe him homage, and attend him in his palaces of Saint Iames, and Sommerset-house'.

Possibly even before the death of his father King James in 1625, Charles set about recruiting new court sculptors. Giambologna's follower, Pietro Tacca, having refused in 1619 to leave his work in Tuscany to produce an equestrian monument of James, Charles was forced to look outside Florence. Perhaps through the influence of his wife, Henrietta Maria, recently arrived from Paris, or through his friend Buckingham, who had been sent to bring the bride home to London, he managed to attract a sculptor who had been in the employ of the French crown, Hubert le Sueur.[5] A portrait medallion by Claude Warin, dated 1635, shows Le Sueur's likeness a decade later, the inscription proudly recording that he was sculptor to two kings (those of France and England) (Fig 1).[6]

The outlines of his career in France are attested by documents, though no sculptures have been attributed to him.[7] Hubert was a son of a master-armourer called Pierre (d 1616), who lived in Paris. He must have been born by 1585 at the latest, for in 1602 he was described as a 'compagnon sculpteur', while at the baptism of his own son in 1610 he was called 'maître-sculpteur'. He was appointed 'sculpteur ordinaire du roi' in 1614, and remained in the royal service until 1624, when his contract was terminated with only half a year's salary. Another document of June 1624 proves that he was winding up his affairs with his Parisian partner, presumably on account of a summons to London.

The constant emphasis in the French royal contracts of employment is on Hubert's ability as a bronze founder:

Sculpteur ayant fait preuve de jecter excellement en bronze toutes sortes de figure.

However, at 300 livres per annum, his retaining fee was distinctly lower than those of other sculptors whose work we know, Dupré, Tremblay or Biard, and this may be a reflection of a humbler status as a skilled foundryman. In this capacity he may have been engaged in casting the four slaves modelled by Francavilla for the base of the equestrian statue of King Henri IV for the Pont Neuf in Paris; this would provide an explanation for the points of contact with the style of Giambologna that have sometimes been noted, for the horse and rider had been cast in Florence by Pietro Tacca and sent to France. Le Sueur could thus have experienced the master's style at second hand through his two best pupils, Francavilla and Tacca, without going to Florence. His contact with the other French court sculptors mentioned above is clearly indicated by the style of his independent sculpture in England.

Le Sueur's first task in London was to produce twelve statues in temporary materials for a funerary catafalque that was 'very ingeniously designed by Mr Inigo Jones' for the late King James.[8] However, his proven ability as a bronze-founder soon secured him commissions for major funereal monuments in Westminster Abbey, the tomb for the Duke of Lennox and Richmond (d 1624), which was in position by 1628;[9] and one for the Duke of Buckingham, who was assassinated in that year.[10] Both are situated in side-chapels off the Chapel of Henry VII in Westminster Abbey. Together they involved the production of a dozen or more life-size statues in bronze, apart from the architectural components and subsidiary ornaments. The effigies of the deceased are the earliest manifestations of Hubert's style as a portraitist: a bland generalised treatment of the facial features is compensated for by an almost obsessive attention to detail in the ladies' dresses and the men's armour – the latter is understandable in view of Hubert's origins in an armourer's family. This is not the place to discuss the complex problems of stylistic origin presented by the allegorical statues on the tombs, which reflect a knowledge not only of French, but German and Netherlandish prototypes.

1 The busts

Whether Le Sueur had been in the King's employment ever since his arrival in England is not known, but he certainly was by 1631, for in that year he was granted the annual rent of £100 for a house and spent four months in Italy taking moulds of ancient

2 *King Charles I* by Le
Sueur, marble, dated 1631
(Victoria and Albert
Museum)

2a   The rear of the socle, with
signature and date

3 *King Charles I* by Le Sueur, bronze, 1636
(Bodleian Library, Oxford)

4 *King Henri IV* by Barthélémy Tremblay, bronze (Musée
Jacquemart-André, Paris)

sculpture at Charles's expense.[11] Bronzes were cast from them for the royal gardens over
the next few years, and some are now in the East Terrace Garden at Windsor Castle.
His earliest datable portrait of King Charles, a weathered but imposing marble bust
now in the Victoria and Albert Museum, was carved in 1631, according to its inscription
(Fig 2).[12] The use of marble is unique among Hubert's portraits and the bust forms a
prototype for a number of bronze variants which were cast in the following years. It is
therefore likely that it was made for the King himself. The hieratic frontality and the
concentration on details of apparel in this bust were typical of Mannerist portraiture in
Northern Europe, though they were rather old-fashioned by current Italian standards.
Not surprisingly, Le Sueur's images of King Charles are indebted to those of Henri
IV.[13] A bust presented by Archbishop Laud to the Bodleian Library, Oxford, in 1636
(Fig 3)[14] is typical of the generality of Le Sueur's bronzes: a comparison with Barthé-
lémy Tremblay's *Henri IV* in the Musée Jacquemart-André, Paris (Fig 4),[15] reveals
the source of the imagery, as well as Hubert's regrettable tendency to simplify the
modelling of the face and hair into a mask and to reduce the lively detailing of a good
French model into a formalised pattern. The motif of lion's masks on the pauldrons –
probably referring to Hercules - is sufficiently unusual in real armour to indicate that
Hubert's source was indeed the bust by Tremblay. Armour of this kind had been made

131

5   *King Charles I* by Le Sueur, bronze, 1637–38
(Chichester Cross)

6   *King Charles I* by Le Sueur, bronze (St Paul's Church,
Hammersmith)

about 1540 for King Francis I of France and may have had a traditional connotation of 'royalty'.[16]

In the late 1630s, when Abraham van der Doort drew up his *Inventory* of the King's collection, two bronze busts by Le Sueur were in the royal collection:[17] 'Done by the ffrenchman – 35. Item . . . the Picture of y[or] Ma[ts] owne selfe in brass soe bigg as the life being onely a head upon a black square, Tutchstone Peddistall'. No such disembodied head has survived, though the heads of most of Le Sueur's portraits were cast separately from the shoulders. Another type of portrait was the subject of an invoice for £60 from Le Sueur in 1636:[18] 'his Majesty's image, with the crown and order well gilt'. The King struck through this item, crossly writing 'This I will not have'! The sculptor subsequently appealed for payment in 1639, leaving the price open:[19] 'Item for y[r] Ma[tes] Pourtraite wth the Imperiall Crowne, wholly guilt (which peece if it should be rejected or neglected would turn to your poore pet(itione)rs great confusion'. The King settled for a modest £30. A bust answering to this description, with the crown and chain of the Order of the Garter, and with traces of gilding, is in an oval recess on the Market Cross in Chichester (Fig 5)[20] while another example, in St Paul's Church, Hammersmith (Fig 6)[21], is adapted for the same accoutrements (which were cast separately in both cases), though they are missing. It is hard to explain the King's

8 *King Charles I's bust at Stourhead* by Michael Rysbrack, after Le Sueur, drawing (Victoria and Albert Museum)

7 *King Charles I* by Le Sueur, gilt bronze, *c* 1636 (National Trust, Stourhead, Wiltshire)

antipathy to this variant of the standard image, unless it was simply to the stiff price which Hubert initially set upon it. However, by 1636 Charles had been portrayed in far more up-to-date fashion by Francois Dieussart[22] and had taken steps to secure a marble bust from Bernini based on the famous triple portrait by Van Dyck (Windsor),[23] so he may well have become aware of the fundamental, aesthetic shortcomings of Hubert's work, for all their elaborate detailing and gilding. These busts are related to the full-length bronze statues of Charles at St John's College, Oxford (1634),[24] at Winchester Cathedral (1638)[25] and one on the new portico added by Inigo Jones to Old St Paul's (destroyed in the Great Fire),[26] all of which showed him in armour, wearing a cloak, cape, and Garter insignia and bearing the full regalia of crown, sceptre and orb.

The third of Le Sueur's designs for portraits of his royal master is known in a unique gilt-bronze now at Stourhead, the recent cleaning of which in the Conservation Department of the Victoria and Albert Museum has occasioned this article (Colour plate XII, Fig 7). Its connection with Le Sueur is proven by its stylistic congruity with his other busts and by the fact that it corresponds with an entry in Van der Doort's catalogue:[27] 'Done by the ffrenchman Lusheere . . . Y. owne Picture cast in brasse wth a helmett upon his head whereon a dragon And a scarfe about the should[rs] soe bigg as the life beeing onely a buske, set upon a – Peddistall made of black Tutchstone.' One manuscript interpolates 'after the Auncient Roman fasshion', after the passage about the

133

9 Armour associated with Geoffrey Hudson
(Royal Armouries, H.M. Tower of London)

10 *King Henri IV* by Matthieu Jacquet, marble (Salle des Gardes, Palais de Fontainebleau)

helmet. The only difference between the Stourhead bust and this description lies in the fact that it has been gilded. While the layer of gilding that has been so strikingly revealed by the cleaning is of considerable age, it may not be contemporary with the casting of the bust. Either Van der Doort mistook the colour for polished brass, or it was added later, perhaps after the Restoration.

It is frustrating that no bust of the King in a helmet is specified among the Commonwealth inventories of sales of the royal possessions, and an entry on a bust at Somerset House sold in 1650, 'The late Kings head in brass' might refer to any of the several bronzes in the royal collection. Vertue first saw it at Stourhead but gave no indication of whence it came or whether its presence there was due to Sir Richard Hoare or to Auditor Benson, his father-in-law. Michael Rysbrack paid tribute to Le Sueur's bust by sketching it carefully in 1733, when he was employed on sculpture for Stourhead (Fig 8).[28] The devices of a dragon on the helmet and a face on the fall appear in actual armour, for example the diminutive suit of early seventeenth-century date associated with Geoffrey Hudson, in the Tower of London (Fig 9), as well as on a famous earlier French royal helmet.[29] Again, Le Sueur's bust is indebted to an earlier portrait of Henri IV, the colossal marble bust now in the central niche over the fireplace of the Salle des Gardes at the palace of Fontainebleau (Fig 10).[30] This masterpiece by Matthieu Jacquet, one of Henri's court sculptors, has an elaborately decorated helmet with a sphinx for its crest;

shows the King's hair curling upwards over the edge of the helmet; and has a square-cut neckline to the breastplate, with the edge of a shirt showing below; while the general shape of the bust is dictated by the catenary folds of the cloak or toga and the classical leather thongs hanging from the pauldrons. All these features appear in Hubert's portrait of Charles. The substitution of a dragon for the sphinx presumably relates to the imagery of St George, which, as we know from Van Dyck's painting of the King as St George, was current in Caroline propaganda. Fanelli's numerous small bronze groups of St George and the dragon, one of which the King owned, are further evidence of the currency of this theme.[31] The use of Roman armour for a contemporary portrait had been pioneered in England by Nicholas Stone in the Francis Holles monument in Westminster Abbey in the 1620s, so Le Sueur was not making a radically new departure.[32] In the case of the King, its use may also reflect contemporary interest in Romano-British culture.[33] If, as seems to be the case, the Stourhead bust was ordered personally by the King, Le Sueur had every reason to excel himself. Indeed, this portrait of his master is the finest that he ever modelled. Probably dating from the late 1630s, it may be regarded as Le Sueur's reply to the appearance in England about 1636–37 of the busts of Charles by his rivals, Dieussart and Bernini.

Plate XII   *King Charles I* by Le Sueur, gilt bronze,
c 1636 (National Trust, Stourhead, Wiltshire)

Having established that Hubert was familiar with the most significant portraits of his earlier royal master, one wonders if he did not himself execute a bust of Henri IV at some stage. In 1610 his Parisian partner, Bourdin, had modelled a head in wax from a death mask.[34] Charles owned a waxen mask of his father-in-law, given him by Abraham van der Doort, according to one manuscript of the inventory, while a head and bust in plaster was listed in the Armoury of St James's under the Commonwealth.[35] A fine, monumental bronze bust showing King Henri IV in plain, contemporary armour, and bare-headed but for a wreath of oak leaves, which is owned by the Duke of Buccleuch, has for some years been on loan to the Victoria and Albert Museum (Fig 11).[36] It conforms to none of the types of portrait associable with Henri's other court sculptors and its provenance is unknown. The technique of casting indicates the seventeenth century and the treatment of surface is like Le Sueur's. The fringed edge of the sash and the decorative pattern of semi-circular leather piccadils round the pauldrons of the armour are common in his portraits, while the cross with the dove of the Ordre de St Esprit appears below the sash at the base of the bust, just where the pendant St George does on Hubert's English knights. The modelling of the face and hair is not so subtle as to preclude Le Sueur as a possible author, for it manifests the level of sensitivity of his best portraits, such as the Stourhead King Charles. The bust may therefore tentatively be included in the *oeuvre* of Le Sueur.

2   The equestrian statuettes

Le Sueur's best known sculpture is the bronze statue of King Charles on horseback in Trafalgar Square (Figs 12, 13).[37] It was commissioned in 1630, not by the King, but by the Lord Treasurer, Sir Richard Weston, for Mortlake Park, Roehampton: the contract makes interesting reading:

> an agreement made with Hubert Le Sueur for the casting of a horse in Brasse bigger than a great Horse by a foot; and the figure of his Maj: King Charles proportionable full six foot, which the aforesaid Hubert Le Sueur is to perform with all the skill and workmanship as lieth in his power . . . of the best yealouw and red copper and carefully provide for the strengthening and fearm opholding of the same, one the pedestal were itt is to stande one, at Roehampton in the right hand the Lord Hey Tresoriers garden. The saide Sueur is also to make a perfect modell of the said Worcke, of the same bigness as the copper shall be, in the making wereof he shall take advice of his Maj: Ridders of greate Horses, as well for the shaepe and action of his Maj: figure one the same.[38]

Le Sueur was to be paid £600 by instalments and took twice as long as the eighteen months stipulated, judging from the date 1633 inscribed with his signature on the baseplate under the left fore-hoof. The equestrian monument had always represented a supreme challenge to sculptors in the classical tradition. The *Marcus Aurelius* on the Capitol at Rome provided proof that such a sculpture was feasible, and both Donatello and Verrocchio had taken up the challenge in the second half of the fifteenth-century.[39] Leonardo da Vinci had failed to bring his monuments to fruition through his over-ambitious intention of having the horse rearing. More recently, in 1591, Giambologna had triumphantly unveiled his monument to Cosimo I de' Medici for the Piazza della Signoria in Florence. This had revived interest in the idea of showing a ruler on horseback, as a supreme tribute to majesty, and all the crowned heads of Europe immediately began to demand such statues from Giambologna or his assistants. The first to be sent

12 and 13 *King Charles I on horseback* by Le Sueur, bronze, dated 1633 (Trafalgar Square, London)

abroad was that of Henri IV for the Pont Neuf in Paris, by Tacca (destroyed in the French Revolution):[40] Le Sueur must have known this example intimately and may have been employed on its ultimate presentation. The connection was not lost on Peacham, who wrote of Le Sueur's project,[41] 'But the great horse with his Majesty on it, twice as great as life, and now well nigh finished, will compare with that of the New Bridge at Paris, or those others at Florence, and Madrid, though made by Sueur his master, John de Bolonia, that rare workman, who not long since lived at Florence.' Lord Treasurer Weston was thus paying the ultimate compliment to his connoisseur-King in commissioning such a monument for his own garden.

Predictably, Hubert was not capable of the finesse which distinguished Giambologna's and Tacca's masterpieces, and one can hardly see the effect of any visits to the royal stables that he may have made in pursuance of the contract. Nevertheless, in the comparatively less sophisticated atmosphere of London in the 1630s, his monument would have made a brave impression. There is a feeling for abstraction in Le Sueur's very broad and bold treatment of form and surface that is appealing: the chunky, resistant quality of cast and chiselled bronze dominates, leaving us in no doubt that this is an idealised image of royalty and not a living portrait of an individual human being, or even an identifiable royal mount.

A number of equestrian statuettes may be convincingly attributed to Le Sueur owing to their morphological and stylistic connection with the monumental statue. Indeed, one depicting the King recently noticed by the author at Ickworth (Figs 14, 15, 16),[43] may have been cast from a small, preliminary model, although there are slight differences in the turn of the horse's head and the angle of its front leg. It may be identical with an item recorded about 1640 by Van der Doort in his inventory of the King's collection, for it is much the same size: '(Done by the ffrenchman) 24. Item yo*r* Ma*ts* owne Picture on horseback upon a black woodden Peddistall belonging to Sommerset house . . . (height: 1 ft 1 in).'[44] The statuette is cast in several sections, as was normal in the Giambologna workshop: head; body and saddle-cloth; horse; tail. The treatment of the head, and especially the mane, of the horse is closely related to Le Sueur's large version, while the armoured figure of the King is in a similar, stiff pose. Interestingly, the miniature version shows him with pauldrons in the shape of lion-masks, which are standard on many of Le Sueur's portrait-busts, though they do not feature on the great equestrian statue.

A statuette in the Royal Collection, purchased only in 1947 from a descendant of Sir John Everett Millais, who had bought it at Christie's, has hitherto been assumed to be the one which belonged to Charles I: the fact that it is gilded, and Van der Doort did not so describe the one he was cataloguing, does not rule out the identification, for, as with the Stourhead bust of King Charles, he may have overlooked the gilding, or it may have been added subsequently. However, in detail it is inferior to the newly-discovered Ickworth version (apart from mere accidents such as the absence of the sword and holder and the clumsy, later fixing of the saddle cloth to the horse). For example, the parallel creases in the horse's neck above its shoulder, and the fringes at the front of the saddle and round the edges of the saddle-cloth are all missing from the Windsor statuette. The head of the King has been completely re-modelled and one wonders if the statuette was cast after the Restoration.

The statuettes are also connected with those produced by Giambologna, Susini and Tacca, which often corresponded with their monumental compositions. For example,

14–16 *King Charles I on horseback* by Le Sueur, bronze statuette (National Trust, Ickworth, Suffolk)

15

16

17 *King Henri IV on horseback* probably by Antonio Susini, bronze statuette (Musée de Dijon)

18 *King Louis XIII on horseback* by Le Sueur, bronze statuette (Victoria and Albert Museum)

a splendid bronze showing Henri IV, now in the Dijon Museum (Fig 17), is the most vivid record of the appearance of the lost statue on the Pont Neuf. Le Sueur almost certainly knew such statuettes, and in any case, the standard *Pacing Horse* (without a rider) by Giambologna, which formed the basis for all the equestrian compositions large or small, was represented in Charles's collection. It had been sent to Prince Henry in 1612 and, when it was unpacked, a courtier had prophetically suggested that it might interest the Duke of York (i.e. Charles), but Henry unkindly refused to give it to him.[45]

It was to Tacca that a fine pair of unusually large statuettes of men in armour on horseback was attributed when given to the Victoria and Albert Museum in 1951 by Dr W. L. Hildburgh.[46] The subjects were not securely identified but are in fact King Henri IV (Fig 23), on a rearing horse, and his son, Louis XIII (Fig 18), their likenesses corresponding perfectly with other portraits. Perhaps owing to uncertainty about the initial attribution (which was justifiably doubted) and their identities, the statuettes were consigned to oblivion. They were resurrected recently by Anthony Radcliffe, when a small bronze statuette of Louis XIII, with the name *LE SVEVR* struck with dies into the girth (Figs 19, 20), appeared at Messrs Sotheby.[47] There was no reason to doubt the authenticity of the signature, and the French subject, who was after all brother-in-law of Charles I, was perfectly consistent with Hubert's early career as court sculptor in Paris. The correspondence of this small statuette with the much larger one in the Museum is close, if allowance is made for differences of proportion due to diverse scales, while both are clearly related to the monument in Trafalgar Square.

19, 20 *King Louis XIII on horseback* by Le Sueur, bronze statuette (London art market 1977)

21, 22 *King Philip III of Spain (?) on horseback* by Le Sueur, bronze statuette (Victoria and Albert Museum)

Another small statuette bequeathed to the Victoria and Albert Museum by Dr Hildburgh fits into the group (Figs 21–22):[48] for the horse and armoured body of the rider are identical with those of the signed statuette of Louis XIII, while the head (which is separately cast with the stiff ruff) is that of King Philip III of Spain. It corresponds approximately with the full-scale equestrian monument manufactured in Florence by Pietro Tacca and sent to Madrid.

The more interesting of Dr Hildburgh's large pair is the statuette showing Henri IV (Fig 23), because of the rearing horse. It indicates that Le Sueur was exploring the same motif as Pietro Tacca, who sent a statuette of a rearing equestrian to Carlo Emmanuele of Savoy about 1621;[49] who produced one of Louis XIII in a curvetting pose for his Medicean relatives in Florence (now in the Bargello); and who ultimately succeeded in producing a full-scale rearing monument to King Philip IV of Spain for Madrid (1634–40).[50] Ironically, Tacca was pipped at the post in this final achievement by Caspar Gras (1585–1674),[51] court-sculptor to the Hapsburgs at Innsbruck, who produced a rearing equestrian statue of the Archduke Leopold V about 1630, following it with a series of statuettes of other archdukes modelled about 1648, one of which is in the Victoria and Albert Museum.[52] Le Sueur seems to have succeeded in overcoming the problem of how to support the weight of the horse and rider by cantilevering through the hind legs into a heavy base. If he produced the bronzes while he was employed by the French crown, ie before 1624, he was abreast of Pietro Tacca; and if during his English period – which cannot be ruled out – he was at any rate in the avant-garde as far as northern Europe was concerned.[53]

Notes

1 The best modern accounts of King Charles's interest in sculpture are: M. D. Whinney and O. Millar, *English Art 1625-1714* (Oxford, 1957), and M. D. Whinney, *Sculpture in Britain 1530-1830* (Harmondsworth, 1964).

2 K. Watson and C. Avery, 'Medici and Stuart: a Grand-Ducal Gift of "Giovanni Bologna" Bronzes for Henry, Prince of Wales (1612)', *Burlington Magazine*, CXV, (1973), pp 493-507.

3 J. Pope-Hennessy, 'Giovanni Bologna's Samson and a Philistine', *Essays on Italian Sculpture* (London, 1968), p 145 f; idem, *Catalogue of Italian Sculpture in the Victoria and Albert Museum*, (London, HMSO, 1964), no. 486; C. Avery, 'Giambologna's Samson and a Philistine', Victoria and Albert Museum *Masterpiece Sheets*, (1978).

4 H. Trevor-Roper, *The Plunder of the Arts in the Seventeenth Century* (London, 1970), pp 28-36; C. V. Wedgwood, 'The Prince of Patrons', *Horizon*, III, 1961, no. 6, pp 79-95. A. Scott-Elliot, 'The Statues from Mantua', *Burlington Magazine*, CI (1959), p 218 f.

5 S. Lami, *Dictionnaire des Sculpteurs de l'école française du Moyen Age au Règne de Louis XIV* (Paris 1898), pp 360-61; Thieme and Becker, *Lexikon der Bildenden Künstler* (Leipzig, 1929), pp 133-34.

6 N. Rondot, *Claude Warin* (extract from *Revue Numismatique* (1888)), pp 29-32, 72-73, cat. no. 75, repro.; D. Piper, *Catalogue of Seventeenth Century Portraits in the National Portrait Gallery* (Cambridge, 1963), no. 939 (electrotype copy).

7 For details of his career in France, I am indebted to communications from Mlle Marie-Antoinette Fleury, Conservateur aux Archives Nationales, Paris, to whom I am most grateful for permission to use her documentary discoveries in advance of her own publication. A complete account of Le Sueur, with detailed citations, is being prepared by the present author for *The Walpole Society*.

23 *King Henri IV on a rearing horse* by Le Sueur, bronze statuette (Victoria and Albert Museum)

8 The literature on Le Sueur's activity in England is as follows and will be cited in abbreviated form as indicated:

H. Walpole/G. Vertue (ed J. Dallaway/R. N. Wornum), *Anecdotes of Painting in England* (London, 1862), II, pp 392-95. = Walpole, *Anecdotes*.

L. Cust, 'A marble bust of Charles I by Hubert Le Sueur', *Burlington Magazine*, XX (1912), pp 192-97. = Cust.

G. Webb, 'Notes on Hubert Le Sueur', *Burlington Magazine*, LII, 1928, pp 10-16. = Webb, I; pp 81-88. = Webb, II.

K. A. Esdaile, 'New light on Hubert Le Sueur', *Burlington Magazine*, LXVI (1935), pp 177-84. = Esdaile (1935).

K. A. Esdaile, 'The busts and statues of Charles I', *Burlington Magazine*, XCI (1949), pp 9-14. = Esdaile (1949).

9 *Calendar of State Papers Domestic, Charles I*, 1628-29, p 329 (17).

10 E. Chamberlayne, *Angliae Notitia*, (1687 edn), pt II, p 303.

11 C. C. Stopes, 'Gleanings from the Records of the Reigns of James I and Charles I', *Burlington Magazine*, XII (1912), p 282. *Cal. S.P.D.*, *CLXXXIII*, *Charles I* (1631), p 491, no. 27.

12 A.35-1910, stated on purchase to have come from Holland. Cust, loc cit.

13 Maumené et d'Harcourt, 'Iconographie des Rois de France', *Archives de l'Art Français*, Nouvelle Periode, XV (1928).

14 R. L. Poole, *A Catalogue of Oxford Portraits* (Oxford, 1939); Royal Commission on Historical Monuments, England, *An Inventory of the Historical Monuments in the City of Oxford* (Oxford, 1939), p 5.

15 P. Vitry and G. Brière, *Documents de Sculpture Française*, Renaissance, II (Paris, 1904), pl CLXXXVI, 2, 5. Paris, Musées Nationaux, *L'Ecole de Fontainebleau* (1972), no. 579.

16 I am grateful to my colleagues Claude Blair and the late Russell Robinson for elucidation. Cf C. Blair, 'Notes on the history of the Tower of London Armouries, 1821-55', *Journal of the Arms and Armour Society*, II, (1956-58), pp 233-53; A. V. B. Norman, 'A note on a Tower armour pedigree', ibid, pp 91-94.

17 O. Millar, 'Abraham van der Doort's Catalogue of the Collections of Charles I', *The Walpole Society*, XXXVII (1958-60), p 97, no. 35.

18 *Cal. S.P.D.*, *CCCXLII*, *Charles I* (1636-37), p 352, no. 97.

19 W. N. Sainsbury, *Original and unpublished papers illustrative of the life of Sir P. P. Rubens* (London, 1859), p 319, Appendix XCIII.

20 My thanks to the Chichester sculptor, Mr Kenneth Child, for kindly erecting a scaffold from which I could examine the bust. Mr Francis Steer has also been most helpful in discussing the historical implications. The inscription, never before noticed, reads: CAROLVS REX. AETAT. XXXVII. It is finely engraved in Roman capitals. The King's age implies that the bust was finished in 1637 or 1638, and it may be identical with one formerly in Charles's collection, but given away by the time Van der Doort wrote his inventory, cf Millar, loc cit, p 40, item 17, and note 4. The best account of the Cross is: W. Steer, 'Bishop Storey and Chichester Cross', *Chichester Papers*, no. 1.

21 Cf C. Bunt, 'A bust of Charles I in chalk-stone', *Apollo* (1931), pp 106-8; Esdaile, loc cit (1949), p 10. Recently refurbished in the Conservation Department of the Victoria and Albert Museum.

22 C. Avery, 'François Dieussart (c 1600-1661), Portrait Sculptor to the Courts of Northern Europe', *Victoria and Albert Museum Yearbook* 4 (1974), pp 65-67.

23 R. Lightbown, 'The Journey of the Bernini Bust of Charles I to England', *The Connoisseur*, CLXIX (1968), pp 217-20.

24 *Cal. S.P.D.*, *Charles I* (1633-34), p 43 (16-17); Poole, op cit, III, pp 168, 172, nos. 35, 46.

25 Sainsbury, op cit, p 319, XCI, XCII. London, Arts Council of Great Britain, *The King's Arcadia* (1973), pp 144-45, no. 256.

26 *The King's Arcadia*, pp 141-43, no. 245.

27 Millar, loc cit, p 70, item 1; Walpole, *Anecdotes*, pp 393-94; Webb, II, p 81; Esdaile (1949), p 10.

28 Victoria and Albert Museum, Department of Prints and Drawings, no. D. 161-1886. Cf M. I. Webb, *Michael Rysbrack, Sculptor* (London, 1954).

29 I am grateful to my colleague Claude Blair for information and the photograph. Cf Niox, *Armes et Armées*, I, *Armure* (Paris), Musee de l'Armée.

30 Ed – J. Ciprut, *Mathieu Jacquet* (Paris, 1967), pl XXXII, Fig 49.

31 J. Pope-Hennessy, 'Some bronze statuettes by Francesco Fanelli', *Essays on Italian Sculpture* (London, 1968), p 166 f.

32 Whinney, pp 26-27, pl 20. W. L. Spiers, 'The Notebook of Nicholas Stone', *The Walpole Society*, VII (1918-19).

33 I am grateful to Dr Roy Strong, Director of the Victoria and Albert Museum, for this observation.

34 Musée Carnavalet, Paris; cf *Apollo*, CI (1975), pp 271-72, Fig 7.

35 Millar, loc cit, p 154, item 4; O. Millar, 'The inventories and valuations of the King's goods, 1649-51', *The Walpole Society*, XLIII (1972), p 156, item 96.

36 My thanks to His Grace the Duke of Buccleuch for his kind permission to publish his bust.

37 Anon, 'The repairs to King Charles's Statue', *Country Life*, (Aug. 2, 1919) pp 133-35; J. G. Mann, 'The Charles I Statue at Charing Cross', *Country Life* (May 16 1947) pp 908-09.

38 *Cal. S.P.D. CLIII, Charles I* (1629-31), p 167, no. 4. Webb, I, p 16.

39 C. Avery, *Florentine Renaissance Sculpture* (London, 1970).

40 The bronze *Slaves*, now in the Louvre are all that survived the French Revolution, apart from some fragments of Tacca's figure of Henri; cf R. de Francqueville, *Pierre de Francqueville* (Paris, 1968).

41 H. Peacham, *The Compleat Gentleman* (London, 1634).

42 J. G. Mann, 'A gilt bronze statuette of King Charles I in the Royal Collection', *The Connoisseur* (*Coronation Book*) (London, 1953), pp 92-96.

43 Probably collection of Frederick Augustus Harvey, 3rd Earl of Bristol and Bishop of Derry (d 1803).

44 Millar, *Van der Doort*, loc cit, p 95.

45 K. Watson and C. Avery, 'Medici and Stuart: a Grand-Ducal Gift of 'Giovanni Bologna' Bronzes for Henry, Prince of Wales', *Burlington Magazine*, CXV (1973), pp 493-507.

46 Nos. A. 49–1951; A. 47–1951.

47 Sotheby, London, 9 December 1976, lot 77.

48 No. A.108-1956, acquired as 'Netherlandish, 17th century'.

49 H. R. Weihrauch, *Europäische Bronzestatuetten*, (Braunschweig 1967), p 231, fig 279.

50 P. Torriti, *Pietro Tacca da Carrara* (Genoa, 1975).

51 E. Egg, 'Caspar Gras und der Tiroler Bronzeguss des 17. Jahrhunderts', *Veröffentlichungen des Museum Ferdinandeum in Innsbruck*, 40 (1960), pp 5-57.

52 No. A. 16–1960.

53 It may be remarked how closely the helmet of Henri IV is related in shape and detail to that of the Stourhead bust of Charles: they share the motif of the dragon-like mask on the fall and the spiral ornament on the sides. Perhaps they reflect real designs from the workshop of Hubert's father, none of whose armour survives.

1 The third Sir Thomas
Lucy (d 1640), a
bibliophile whose
monument in Charlecote
church has shelves of
books carved behind his
effigy

The Lucys of Charlecote and their Library

HENRY SUMMERSON

Untrustworthy legend would have us believe that Sir Thomas Lucy of Charlecote in Warwickshire did as much for English literature as any man in its history when he drove the young William Shakespeare, who had lampooned him after being caught poaching his deer, from obscurity in Stratford to glory at the Globe. Be the truth of this story what it may,[1] there can be no doubt that successive generations of Lucys took an interest in literature that went beyond harassing into prominence its greatest practitioner, for they bought books, read them, even made notes in them, and the library at Charlecote today stands witness to the reading tastes of the Lucys and of the families they intermarried with over more than four centuries.

The library can first be seen as a whole in June 1681, when there was made 'A Catalogue of the Books in Charlcot studdy'.[2] This records 1266 titles and over 1400 volumes, divided into nine sections, Law Books (109 titles), French Books (289), Physick Books (39), Philosophy Books (29), History and Books of Polite Literature (286), School Books and Classick Authors (107), and three sections of Divinity Books (407). The entries in the catalogue are always brief and often obscure. Trenchant entries like 'Against Puritanisme' and 'Contra Independents' leave no doubt about the contents of the books they record, but, by omitting such mundane details as authors' names and full titles, leave them unidentifiable. The reason for this will have lain in seventeenth-century book arrangement. Books were usually placed on shelves with their fore-edges, not their spines, facing out into the room, and their titles written across or down their fore-edges, sometimes in full, more often abbreviated. The cataloguer in 1681 probably simply noted down what was written on the fore-edges. The catalogue naturally does not say who owned all these books. Of course one can make an occasional guess. No doubt it was the Thomas Lucy who was sewer to Henry VIII[3] who loyally bought that monarch's *Assertio Septem Sacramentorum,** while many of the classical texts will have belonged to the third Sir Thomas Lucy, whose monument in Charlecote church actually has four shelves of books, some with titles, carved behind his effigy – they include a 1579 edition of Homer's *Iliad* and Xenophon carved in Greek letters. But the seventeenth-century library is best considered as a whole, for the light it sheds on the tastes and interests of a succession of intelligent and cultivated country squires.

On the whole, the reading tastes of the Lucys were in keeping with those of their class and age,[4] as the first section of the catalogue, that of Law Books, demonstrates. To be at least as much concerned with legal theory and history as with practice was quite usual in the seventeenth century, and so alongside Fitzherbert's *New Boke of Justices of the Peas** and Michael Dalton's *The Country Justice*, books which one might expect to find on any J.P.'s shelves, there stood the works of Glanville,* Bracton and Britton, the *Codex Justiniani* and a *Decretale*, and the Statutes of most of the English monarchs between Edward III and Charles I. While the possession of books suggesting a belief that there was more to law than the preservation of game and the chastisement of vagrants was intellectually fashionable, the Lucys may of course have been genuinely broadminded, the result perhaps of university education or foreign travel. The second Sir Thomas Lucy, who was a friend of Francis Bacon, owned French and Italian books[5] and may have gone abroad. His son, the third Sir Thomas, certainly went to France,[6] where he fought duels and bought books – Regnier's *Satires*, Vigenère's translation of

Philostratus*, d'Aubigné's *Aventures du Baron de Faeneste*, all published early in the seventeenth century, no doubt came back with him to Charlecote. At least one of his sons, too, appears to have gone to France, and to have bought Tassin's *Plans et Profils de toutes les principales Villes et Lieux considerables de France** to help him find his way about. It was published in 1638, by which time Sir Thomas was too old to travel again. Perhaps it was his second son Robert, the owner of a French bible,* who went.

In their choice of books of divinity the Lucys again showed a breadth of interests which, perhaps surprisingly, was far from unusual at the time. Religious toleration was not a common virtue in the sixteenth and seventeenth centuries, and the Lucys may well have held to their own religious views as strongly as anybody, but, like other serious-minded people, they took the trouble to make themselves familiar with the views they rejected. Certainly their library contained a very wide range of theological opinions. Probably this was mainly due to Lady Alice Lucy, wife of the third Sir Thomas, of whom her funeral sermon said 'A great librarie shee had, wherein were most of our choicest English Authors. No sooner could shee hear of anie pious Book made publick, but she endevored to make it hers, and her self the better for it.'[7] This claim is fully borne out by the catalogue. Among continental authors, the works of the Catholic cardinals Bellarmine and Baronius kept company with those of Luther, Calvin and Beza, books by the Dutch Protestant Hugo Grotius with the official publication of the Jesuits, *Regulae Jesuitarum*, and the *De Imitatione Christi* of Thomas à Kempis. English authors are both more numerous and easier to identify, and here too the keynote is variety. Orthodox Anglicans like Richard Hooker and Thomas Fuller are listed beside the Brownist Henry Jacob and the Scottish Presbyterian Robert Baillie. *A Treatise of the Divine Promises* by Edward Leigh, who was a colonel in the Parliamentary army in the Civil War, stood on the same shelves as the sermons of John Hewett, beheaded in 1658 for his share in a royalist conspiracy. There were even two books by Richard Baxter, a non-conformist regarded with suspicion by all right-thinking people – perhaps these were bought in the spirit which made some later Lucy write on the fly-leaf of Baxter's *Gildas Salvianus* 'even a bad man may sometimes think and speak good things'! An interesting feature of the library was the number of works in it by Catholic authors. In the years of Babington's Conspiracy and the Gunpowder Plot the Lucys were buying books by Robert Parsons, who argued that the king of Spain was by lawful inheritance also king of England, and by Laurence Vaux and Roger Widdrington, both Catholic priests who died in English prisons. It must not be thought, however, that because the Lucys were tolerant in their reading tastes the books themselves were tolerant. On the contrary, most of them were typical products of an age which required that in the cause of religious controversy no punches should be pulled and no holds barred. Titles like Matthew Sutcliffe's *Examination . . . of a Scurrilous Treatise published by Mr Kellison* and John Darrell's *Detection of that Sinful, Shameful, Lying and Ridiculous Discours of Samuel Harshnett* convey the gist of their contents with a brutal succinctness that almost makes it unnecessary to read the books.

In their 'books of history and polite literature' as in their religious books, the Lucys were at one with their age, this time in its confused attitude to science, in its inability to distinguish the valuable from the worthless. Their library contained such works as Cabeo's *Philosophia Magnetica* and Robert Boyle's *New Experiments Physico-Mechanicall touching the Spring of the Air*, but it also contained the *Malleus Maleficarum* of Kramer and Sprenger, Remy's *Demonolatrie* and Christopher Heydon's *Defence of Judicial*

2 A selection of books from the Charlecote library catalogued in 1681, seen as they would have been arranged in the seventeenth century, with the titles written on their fore-edges

Astrology. The great Kepler was indeed represented on its shelves, but only by his *Harmonice Mundi*, a rather cranky work which set out to prove that certain geometrical proportions were omnipresent in the universe and had guided the hand of God in the work of Creation. Of Galileo and Descartes, William Harvey and Isaac Barrow, there is no discernible mention. Other books, too, dealing with other subjects, were also conspicuous by their absence. Hobbes's *Leviathan* was one, though books attacking its author were listed. Raleigh's *History of the World*, Milton's *Paradise Lost*, Browne's *Religio Medici*, Coke's *Institutes* and the *Eikon Basilike* all went unread at Charlecote. And one name greater than these was also missing. Several books by Warwickshire men were bought by the Lucys – the poems of Michael Drayton, the epigrams of John Owen, even *England's Improvement* in which Andrew Yarrenton argued that Stratford-upon-Avon would make an ideal centre for the mum trade. But of Shakespeare there is no mention. The voice of the sweet swan of Avon, though delightful to 'Eliza and our James', seems to have had no charms at Charlecote. Perhaps he really had lampooned the first Sir Thomas after all.

The tone of the library as a whole was a serious one, and light reading, even by seventeenth-century standards, took up little space in it. If *Clidamas* or *Nyssena: a Romance* failed to appeal, the satires of John Barclay or the exploits of Amadis de Gaul, in eight volumes, all in French, may have had to provide entertainment. Only one play, listed simply as *A Comedy*, can be identified in the whole collection. This state of affairs continued for a while after 1681. Thomas Lucy, a member of Parliament and Captain of the Horse who lived a gay and fashionable life in London[8] before his early death in 1684, collected tracts relating to the Popish Plot and possessed Speed's *History of Great Britaine** and Allestree's *Causes of the Decay of Christian Piety*, while his cousin Davenport, who succeeded him as owner of Charlecote, owned and presumably

151

3　Dr William Lucy (d 1723), who reorganised the library in the early eighteenth century

4　The third Sir Thomas Lucy's copy of Moreau's *Tableau des Armoiries de France*, with his initials tooled on its cover. It was repaired by Dr William Lucy

read Stillingfleet's *Discourse concerning the Idolatry practised in the Church of Rome*, before being killed at the siege of Limerick in 1690. Davenport's brother and successor George does not appear to have cared much for books himself, for he only wrote his name into one book, Worlidge's *Systema Agriculturae*, and spelt it Gorg, but his marriage brought to Charlecote a collection of books from outside. In 1697 he married Mary Bohun, daughter of John Bohun of Finham, a Coventry merchant and a staunch Protestant – more a Dissenter than an Anglican, as the pathetic note on the fly-leaf of his copy of Clarkson's *Primitive Episcopacy* reveals:

> The author of these 2 excellent Treatises (one of ye most learned and humble persons that ever I had ye Happiness to be acquainted with) hath in them overthrown Hierarchy & Liturgy (and what more is ye Church of England?) so farr as Arguments can do it. But ye Belly wants ears. Thy Kingdom come! I will effectualy perform it in God's time, Amen!

John Bohun's books, left by him to his daughter,[9] reflect these stern religious views – books like Caryl's *Exposition upon the Book of Job*, Ferguson's *Interest of Reason in Religion*, Rogers' *Renunciation of Several Popish Doctrines* – and can only have deepened the already austere tone of the library.

Mary Bohun died in 1708, and four years later George Lucy married her cousin Jane Bohun. Husband and second wife had extravagant tastes – George lost £3,000 in the South Sea Bubble[10]– and, though family feeling may have kept the Bohun books out of the dealers' hands, it was probably now, to pay off gambling debts, that the dispersal of the seventeenth-century library began. Certainly George's successor at Charlecote, his brother Dr William Lucy, seems to have set about reorganising the library. The 1684 edition of Foxe's *Book of Martyrs*, which replaced that listed in 1681,

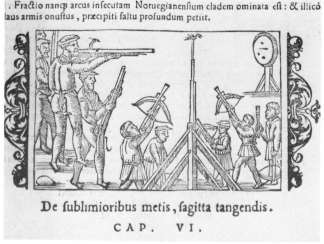

5   The Rev John Hammond, who was a fanatical collector of books, and whose library came to Charlecote with his son in 1787

6   A woodcut from the Rev John Hammond's copy of the *Historia de Gentibus Septentrionalibus of Olaus Magnus*. Another copy of this book had been at Charlecote in 1681

was bought by him, while Moreau's *Tableau des Armoiries de France,** with the third Sir Thomas Lucy's initials tooled on its early seventeenth-century green morocco gilt binding, received new endpapers and Dr William's bookplate. Dr William's own taste in books was catholic. Plenty of theology, as befitted a clergyman – Bennet's *Confutation of Popery*, Calvin's *Institutio Christianae Religionis*, Wall's *History of Infant-Baptism* found places on his shelves. He read history in the shape of Clarendon's *History of the Rebellion* and Burnet's *History of His Own Times*, and he had a liking for travel books, buying Frezier's *Voyage to the South Sea* and Crull's *Antient and Present State of Muscovy*. His political views are indicated by his ownership of the notorious Mrs Manley's *New Atalantis*, in which the Whig ministers directing the War of the Spanish Succession were libelled with rabid indecency, and he had an eye to his own domestic comfort, since he bought Nott's *Cook's and Confectioner's Dictionary*.

William's manifest exuberance of personality was not matched by his wife, Frances Balguy. In the light of her inability to bear a child, her possession of *The Lady's New Year Gift or Advice to a Daughter* is pathetic. But that her nature was basically joyless is shown by the fact that while still unmarried she received from her future husband *The Mystery of Phanaticism or the Artifices of the Dissenters to support their Schism*, surely one of the most lugubrious courting presents on record. A lighter note is provided by the Reverend Thomas Coney, who as rector of Chedzoy in Somerset had been William Lucy's neighbour when the latter was rector of Tolland, also in Somerset. In 1722 he dedicated his *The Devout Soul* to William, prefacing his text with a dedicatory letter of cringing servility –

And permit me sir [he concludes] to add further upon this Head, That your constant Zeal in espousing my Interest, as often as there was occasion for a Proctor in

Convocation, and your wonderful Humility and Condescension, in designing to accept me for your Colleague at the next Election, is what shall always be remember'd with Pleasure and mention'd with Gratitude, by, Reverend Sir, your most Humble and Most Obedient Servant, Tho. Coney.[11]

The Reverend William Collins could hardly have put it better.

Dr William Lucy owned Charlecote for only two and a half energetic years, dying childless in 1724, when his heir, his nephew Thomas, was only twelve years old. An epileptic, Thomas died in 1744, leaving Charlecote to his younger brother, George. George Lucy was not really bookish. He wrote his name into Frances Lucy's copy of Collins's *Peerage of England*, and he bought Nelson's *Laws of England concerning the Game of Hunting, Hawking, Fishing and Fowling* – no doubt he shared the strong views of his forbears on the heinousness of poaching. But if he didn't read much himself, he remained aware of his responsibilities to the family library, and so he bought books by subscription. It may well be that Jago's *Edge Hill* and Ballard's *Memoirs of Several Ladies . . . celebrated in the learned languages arts and sciences* remained unopened from the moment of their arrival, but had it not been for George Lucy's conscientiousness they would never have found places on the library shelves at all.

When George Lucy died in 1786, unmarried, Charlecote passed to his cousin John Hammond, who at once took the name of Lucy. With him another family library came to Charlecote, collected principally by his father, also John Hammond, who had succeeded William Lucy as rector of Tolland and who carried the pursuit of books to what seem quite excessive lengths. A note in his copy of Ken's *Exposition on the Church Catechism*, 'Bought of Widow Daw of Sarr being one of her late sons. Cost 2s 6d', suggests that the parishioners of Tolland might reasonably have numbered among the

7   George Lucy (d 1845), who built the present Library at Charlecote and bought books to fill it

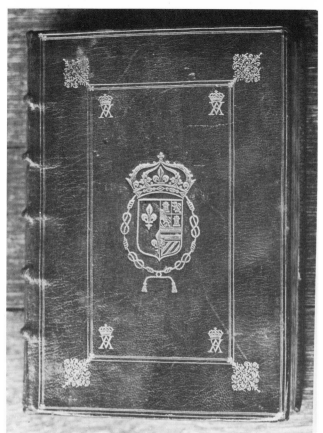

8 A painting of the Tudor coat-of-arms inserted into a copy of Erasmus' *Institutiones Principis Christiani* presented to Henry VIII. George Lucy bought this book in 1838

9 Anne of Austria's copy of De Coste's *Eloges des Dames Illustres*, bought by George Lucy in 1838

horrors of bereavement visits from the rector, come not to administer comfort but to hunt for bargains for his library. Whatever their source, the Hammond collection contained some notable books. Milton's *Paradise Lost*, with the eighth title page of 1669, Melancthon's edition of Terence of 1528, Stafforde's *Brief Description of the Whole World* of 1617, and a first edition of Bacon's *De Augmentis Scientiarum* came to Charlecote now, together with copies of a few books which had been in the library in 1681 but had since gone elsewhere, the *Historia de Gentibus Septentrionalibus* of Olaus Magnus, *De Vita* by Fortunius Licetus, Godwin's *Moses and Aaron* and Crakanthorp's *Defensio Ecclesiae Anglicanae*. Having brought these and many other volumes to his new home, John Hammond Lucy proceeded to ignore them. His own name has been found in only two books, and these, as one would expect with a clergyman, were both devotional. He may even have sold some both of his father's books[12] and of such books as survived from the seventeenth-century Lucy collection. When he died in 1823 the books at Charlecote were valued at only £438 6s 6d,[13] less than had been spent on George Lucy's funeral nearly forty years earlier.[14]

John Lucy's wife Maria possessed a copy of Bishop Percy's *Reliques of Ancient Poetry*, which suggests that she shared the late eighteenth century's new feeling for the romantic and picturesque. Were this so, she certainly passed this taste on to her son George, a true-blue romantic who one feels sure would have taken part in the Eglinton tournament had he only been born a peer instead of a squire, and who with his wife Mary Elizabeth set about restoring Charlecote to what he thought of as its ancient splendours with a whole-hearted disregard for historical niceties, which resulted in its becoming one of the finest examples in England of Victorian Tudor architecture.[15] A new library was a prominent part of this refurbishment, and once it was built new books had to be bought and old books repaired or rebound so that its shelves should be worthily filled. A few books came into the new library as gifts, though these varied as to literary quality, Lord Leigh presenting two volumes of his own poems, whereas Elias Webb gave a Shakespeare second folio. But for the most part books had to be paid for, and William Pickering of Chancery Lane in London was the bookseller to whom George Lucy turned most often and who received most of the £772 7s 9d he spent on books.[16]

It is hard to see any pattern in George Lucy's book-buying other than a desire to have books in keeping with a noble house. That it was the appearance and titles of books as much as their contents which concerned him is suggested by a list Pickering sent him of mainly seventeenth century books 'worth next to nothing from their very bad state', a description that may well turn the modern collector green, since it covers such volumes as *Reliquiae Wottonianae* 1651, John Evelyn's *Sylva* 1664, and the second edition of Hobbes's *History of the Civil Wars*. However, George's conscience forbade him to buy crumbling books solely for the sake of their bindings, and in the end he and Pickering contrived to bring some remarkable books to Charlecote at prices which seem today to have been amazingly low. A first edition of the *Workes* of Sir Thomas More, for ten guineas, a copy of the *Institutiones Principis Christiani* of Erasmus prepared for presentation to Henry VIII, for £3 13s 6d, a second quarto of Shakespeare's *Merry Wives of Windsor*, for six guineas, Anne of Austria's copy of De Coste's *Eloges des Dames Illustres*, for one guinea. These are only a few of the treasures that George Lucy acquired. Of course such books were bought primarily for show. In his leisure hours one imagines he did not settle down with the Tertullian that had once been Ben Jonson's or work his way through nine volumes of Leland's *Itinerary*. Early in 1839 he bought all the novels of Jane Austen, and these, perhaps, took his mind off his rotten borough and the new stained-glass windows. Certainly it is pleasant to think of George Lucy, who, as his wife wrote, 'was fond of the study of heraldry and took great pains in tracing the pedigree of his ancestors',[17] drawing up to the fire to read about Sir Walter Elliot and Lady Catherine de Burgh.

With George Lucy's death in 1845, hard times set in for Charlecote, during which house and estate bravely kept up appearances in the face of financial difficulties largely caused by George's extravagance. In the library a number of mostly unimportant books came in and a few rare and valuable books departed via dealers or auction rooms. For the additions it was the women of the family who were largely responsible, perhaps because reading was one of the few ways social convention allowed them to amuse themselves. George's son and heir, William Fulke Lucy, survived his father by only three years and had little chance to contribute anything to the library beyond his school textbooks and prizes and a copy of E. B. Mardon's *Billiards*, while his younger brother and successor at Charlecote, Henry Spencer Lucy, in between reading the *Newgate Calendar*, does not seem to have cared much about anything except sport. But the ladies – George's widow Mary Elizabeth, Henry Spenser's wife Christina Campbell and their daughter Ada Christina – were a lot livelier. Mary Elizabeth wrote a good deal herself – for private circulation only – notably a history of the Lucys, and she bought the scandalous Mrs Norton's *Child of the Islands* and *Soeur Anne* by the rather risqué Paul de Kock. Christina read Schiller in German and went in for science, buying

10 An early photograph of the Library at Charlecote, built for George Lucy

Darwin's *Origin of Species*, which she may have read, and Lyell's *Geological Evidences of the Antiquity of Man*, which she certainly did not, the pages remaining uncut to this day. Her daughter Ada did very little better with Carey's translation of Dante, failing to reach the end of the *Inferno*, but she also owned the novels of George Eliot and Ruskin's *Modern Painters*, as well as books about the history and topography of Warwickshire, and perhaps these are a truer indication of her literary tastes.

By the end of the nineteenth century, books, like pictures, were being sold to fuel the battle against taxation and the fall in the value of agricultural land. The books that went, though few, were choice. A Missal bearing the signatures of Henry VII, Elizabeth of York, Henry VIII, Katherine of Aragon and Bloody Mary, sold to George Lucy by Pickering in 1839 for £75 and described by him as 'quite unique', was sold immediately after George's death.[18] Others followed later. Six volumes of Molière, bought for five guineas in 1838, fetched £250 exactly a hundred years later. When Mascal's *Book of Fishing with Rod and Line* of 1599, Diane de Poitiers' copy of Gesner's *Historia Animalium*, with her coat-of-arms on its cover, bought for ten guineas in 1838, and other sixteenth- and seventeenth-century volumes left Charlecote is not recorded. In spite of these losses, the Charlecote library today is much the same as it was when George Lucy died. In some ways this is unfortunate, since to George his library was basically a collector's showpiece, where fine bindings beguiled the eye and the rarity of some of its contents obscured the fact that the books in it seldom left their shelves, whereas before his time, although the books may frequently have been in disorder and the temptation to turn some of them into money was occasionally irresistible, they

157

were essentially meant to be read. As such, not only do they reflect the personalities of those who owned them, the seriousness of the sixteenth- and seventeenth-century Lucys, Dr William's vigour and vitality, John Hammond's bibliomania; they also show that for generations members of a single Warwickshire family, rarely of more than local consequence, were as likely to have a book in their hands as a hunting crop or a fishing rod, and prove, for those who need such proof, that at no time in the past did rural seclusion constitute a bar to the pursuit of intellectual interests.

The Lucy Family

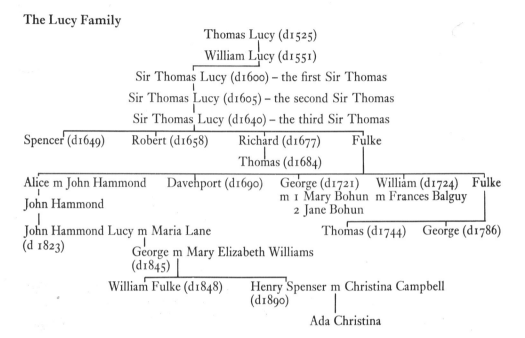

Acknowledgments
I am grateful for advice and assistance from Alice, the Hon Lady Fairfax-Lucy, Mr Edward Miller and, in particular, Mr and Mrs O. J. Pattison of Charlecote Park, without whose help and hospitality this article could never have been written. I am also indebted to the labours of others who have worked in the library at Charlecote, in particular to the notes left by the Hon Robert Gathorne-Hardy, Dr Robert Birley, Mr C. E. R. Clarabut and Mr C. R. N. Routh.

Notes

1 See Alice Fairfax-Lucy, *Charlecote and the Lucys* (Oxford, 1958), pp 3-12, 81-85.

2 This catalogue was very badly damaged by floods in 1947. Fortunately, a transcript had been made in 1940 by Mr Philip Styles, and it is this which I have used, together with notes made by Styles and Mr C. E. R. Clarabut. Certain identification of books listed in this catalogue is not always possible, but about one hundred of the books recorded in 1681 are still in the library.

3 *Charlecote and the Lucys*, p 318.

4 For advice on this point I am grateful to Mr Edward Miller, the National Trust's Libraries Adviser.

5 *Charlecote and the Lucys*, pp 102, 106.

6 op cit, pp 119-20.

7 Thomas Dugard, *Death and the Grave: or a Sermon Preached at the Funeral of that Honorable and Virtuous Ladie, the Ladie Alice Lucie, August 17th 1648* (London 1649), p 46.

8 *Charlecote and the Lucys*, pp 164-70.

9 Warwick Record Office L6/1221.

10 *Charlecote and the Lucys*, pp 181-84.

11 Thomas Coney, *The Devout Soul*, (London, 1722), p ix.

12 Suggested by a note on the fly-leaf of John Hammond's copy of R. Wensley's *The Form of Sound Words...* (London, 1679) listing another twelve books bought at the same time, of which only two can be said with certainty to be still in the library. What is known of John Hammond argues that he would be the last person to sell off his own books.

13 Warwick Record Office L6/1527.

14 *Charlecote and the Lucys*, p 238.

15 op cit Chapter 7; 'Elizabethan-Revival Charlecote Revived' by John Hardy and Clive Wainwright in *National Trust Yearbook 1976-77*, pp 12-19.

16 All the details of George Lucy's book buying are to be found in Warwick Record Office L6/1145.

17 Mary Elizabeth Lucy, *The Lucys of Charlecote* (privately printed, 1862) p 164.

18 In 1846 it was in the collection of the Rev William Maskell, and passed to the British Museum the following year. It is now Additional MS 17012 in the Department of Manuscripts, the British Library. Information from Mr Edward Miller.

1   The Chapel at Knole, near Sevenoaks. Built by Archbishop Bourchier in the
late fifteenth century, though with pews and pulpit installed by the 1st Earl of
Dorset, *c* 1605–8

Music at Knole

WYN K. FORD

The present house at Knole traces its history from 1456, when it was purchased from Lord Say, the constable of Dover Castle, by the Archbishop of Canterbury, Thomas Bourchier.[1] The Archbishop seems to have been 'devoted to music',[2] but there is no evidence that he was ever actively involved with the art.[3] He lavished attention on the fabric of the house and spent much time there,[4] but there is nothing to suggest any special musical activity at this time, although the archbishop would have maintained a group of musicians to perform the various offices in the chapel (Fig 1). The house was enlarged by Bourchier's successor, John Morton, who entertained Henry VII there,[5] and Archbishop Warham spent much time at the house during his archiepiscopate (1503-33); but again there is little sign of musical activity, although Warham was addicted to entertaining cultured folk at meals during which music would have been played.[6]

Not until 1538 can we discern anything of a musical tradition at Knole. In January 1537/38 one Walter Hendle had visited the house to declare its transfer to the King from Cranmer.[7] The situation of the estate appealed to Henry VIII as healthy; as he grew older his tendency to hypochondria was becoming more pronounced, and he declared, 'I myself will lye at Knolle'.[8]

Unfortunately he does not seem to have paid many visits to the house, although frequent payments were made for its upkeep and enlargement. Only once in the two years from September 1538 did the king's retinue visit Kent, and then only across the north of the county, in March 1538/39.[9] There seem to have been only three occasions, two in 1541, in which Knole figured in the King's projected itineraries: in passing from Otford to Penshurst during the summer, and again from Greenwich to Penshurst; the third list is undated, but from the same period: again the court is passing from Otford to Penshurst. A little later, in 1544, a payment is recorded to Hugh Lighe for spending three days in searching 'for sickness' at Otford and Knole as well as at the palaces of Greenwich and Eltham. But whether any of these visits actually materialised does not appear.[10]

Henry's musical abilities are well known.[11] The achievements of his youth seem to have been particularly impressive,[12] but towards the end of his life his powers waned, and in 1541 he suffered from a severe depression for a time, losing his taste for the art, although his interest remained with him to the end of his life.[13] The performance of the Chapel Royal was especially admired by foreign visitors, and the King ordained that members of its should be in constant attendance.[14] We may therefore suppose that a body of singers accompanied him on any visit he made to Knole, especially in view of his interest in liturgical music. Perhaps John Heywood, his virginalist, was also in his retinue. But all this is mere supposition.

After the King's death the ownership of Knole passed through several hands. Cardinal Pole had it for two and a half years before his death in 1558.[15] He has been described as 'unworldly' and as exhibiting 'the Renaissance at its best',[16] and we may imagine that under him Knole reverted for a time to its former glories.

In 1561 Knole passed to Robert Dudley, Earl of Leicester, for five years. The magnificence of his entertainment of the Queen at Kenilworth later in 1575 is well known;[17] it included much music-making when she arrived, and we may suppose that he had some liking for the art. It seems that Peter Lupo, later a member of the royal music for forty years, first found employment among his retainers, who included also a company of players.[18]

The Queen herself stayed at the house for five days in July, 1573. The household accounts[19] show that on an earlier progress that year she left the *famillia*, or household, at Greenwich. But there is no indication that she did so on this occasion, and it seems that her whole retinue accompanied her. The musicians among them were preponderantly trumpeters, with sackbuts, drummers and flautists, and a single violist and lutanist.[20] She herself, like her father, was no mean singer and player, although it seems she performed only in private.[21] If at the time Knole was still 'her own house',[22] she would have been spared the interminable entertainments staged by her hosts elsewhere; dancing, domestic music and perhaps music at mealtimes sufficed, together with music in the chapel around which the life of the house revolved.[23]

Hasted's account of the estate after Leicester had relinquished it is rather involved. But he makes it clear[24] that John Lennard of Chevening took up residence in the house between 1570 and 1574. Lennard had been prominent in local affairs for some time: he had been appointed to the commission for the peace in 1562, and in 1566 he was in the running for appointment as sheriff, having already become *custos brevium*.[25]

With the Lennard family we come across Knole's first definite link with music. In 1590 John Baldwin of Windsor wrote out an anthology of keyboard pieces by William Byrd called *My Ladye Nevells Booke*, which eventually found its way into the queen's possession. It has been suggested[26] that this Lady Nevell may be identified with Rachel, daughter of John Lennard. As the identification has been questioned,[27] some circumstantial evidence that seems to have been overlooked may be advanced in support of it.

At that time the lord of the neighbouring manor of Sevenoaks was Henry Carey, Lord Hunsdon; the Queen had granted it to him in 1558/59, and she had given him additional rights connected with it in 1571; furthermore, in May that year, he obtained a market charter for Tonbridge.[28] It seems reasonable to suppose that this part of Kent attracted him more than his other estates; its proximity to the royal palaces of Greenwich and Westminster would have been an added attraction to the lord chamberlain. In that capacity, Lord Hunsdon had shown favour to Byrd, and in gratitude the composer had dedicated to him his *Songs of Sundrie Natures* in 1589, two years before *My Ladye Nevells Booke* was finished.[29]

Lord Hunsdon died in 1596, and was succeeded by his son, George, whose interest in music was more marked. George was a patron of both Morley and John Dowland, and the latter dedicated to him his *First Booke of Songes* in 1597; the collection included the 'Lord Chamberlain's galliard', a piece written presumably for George.[30] The second Lady Hunsdon was Elizabeth Spencer of Althorp, of a family with pronounced musical and literary interests.[31] Very probably it was for her that Dowland wrote an allemande for lute, 'My Lady Hunsdon's Puffe', about 1610.[32] We thus have grounds for suggesting that there was at this period a cultural climate favourable to music in the vicinity of Knole; not until after 1609 did the Carey family give up its interests in Sevenoaks.[33]

In 1603 or later the lease of the house to the Lennard family expired, and the estate reverted to Thomas Sackville, Lord Buckhurst, who was created Earl of Dorset in 1604.[34] In his youth he had been a considerable poet: among his works are the two acts he contributed to the tragedy *Gorboduc*, the performance of which involved music.[35]

2 The screen in the Great Hall at Knole, probably made, *c* 1608, by the King's carpenter, William Portinton. The minstrels' gallery is at the top, behind a grille

In this also he may have been involved; four years afterwards he brought over from the Continent as his servant one William de Man, who is plausibly identified with Damon, to become a royal musician, whose surviving compositions consist almost entirely of liturgical and devotional music, notably settings of metrical psalm tunes.[36] Lord Buckhurst was clearly attracted to music, in which above all he seems to have found recreation after the cares of daily life.[37] That subsequent members of the family were also interested in the art is suggested by the presence of documents concerning the wellbeing of musicians elsewhere among the family papers.[38]

Lord Dorset's surviving accounts for 1604–8 show that he was then spending very considerable sums on the house;[39] we notice that the imposing screen in the great hall,[40] with a minstrels' gallery above (Fig 2), dates from this period. We learn also the names of some at least of his musicians at this time.[41] Most are merely names; others joined the court, and thus we have further details of them. Ten of them received wages due to them at the time of the earl's death: Bonadventure Ashby may perhaps be identified with John Ashby, who was named with 'Mr Myners' as a musician in 1612 at Prince Henry's funeral.[42] John Miners is also shown as 'one of your Lordship's Musitians', not as receiving wages, but as being reimbursed for 'strings bought for your lordship's Violls and Violins' on two separate occasions. He was a member of the prince's household, and joined the choir of Exeter Cathedral only to quit it immediately for the Chapel Royal just before he died in 1615.[43]

Besides the two who apparently were singers, we can identify instrumentalists with a fair degree of probability. Horatio Lupo was one of the court musicians between about 1611 and 1626;[44] he played the violin,[45] and probably the viol also. Another future Royal musician was Jonas Wrench, who was one of the King's chamber musicians for 'lutes, violls and voices' in 1625 and until his death towards the close of 1626; probably his service was considerably longer than the records suggest, since his name was still appearing thirty-six years after his death.[46] Thomas White seems to have entered the service of the King of Poland, in 1617, at the outbreak of war with Sweden.[47] On the slight evidence available, it seems that the Knole musicians displayed considerable versatility in the range of their expertise.

As to the sources from which the family obtained its domestic musicians, we can only speculate. Jonas Wrench very possibly came from Gloucestershire or East Anglia, since the surname was current there.[48] Baptist Larkin, of whom we know nothing, may have been related to William Larkin, a painter patronised by the family ten years later.[49]

The most tantalising of all, however, is William Symmes. He is described in the accounts as 'late one of your Lordship's Musitians' when he was paid off on 19 March 1608, a fortnight before the ten others had their wages. He is one of those shadowy figures in English music of the period, a composer of whom virtually nothing is known. He wrote both chamber music and anthems;[50] he has been ranked as one of 'Thomas Ford's spiritual relatives', with other little-known composers.[51] An anthem of his was included in *Tristitiae Remedium*, a collection of sacred music assembled in 1616 by a divine named Thomas Myriell, to which Thomas Lupo also contributed;[52] the nature of the surviving sources suggests that his anthems were designed for private devotion rather than liturgical use. Such indications as there are suggest a Kentish origin for him;[53] but where he went after leaving Knole remains a mystery. And perhaps we shall never know how much of his music was written by that time.

Talented though his own musicians undoubtedly were, the accounts show that Lord Dorset called upon outside help when the need arose. On 7 January Thomas Cordwell was paid 'for the hire of him and the rest of his company of violins' at Christmas. We have no further details save that he received five pounds, a quarter's wages for one of his lordship's own musicians, and the amount paid under similar circumstances in the summer of 1613 by another great man for seventeen days' service. Such practices were not unusual,[54] but Cordwell was no itinerant minstrel: in all probability he was the same as the Thomas Cordall who was among the 'lutes and others' receiving mourning livery for the Queen's funeral in 1603.[55]

Such is the brief glimpse we have of musical activity at Knole at the end of Thomas Sackville's life. It is manifestly incomplete: there is no mention of payment of wages to John Miners, and we have little information about most of the musicians beyond their names. Even so, it is by no means certain that we have succeeded in identifying all who played music in the house; there is no mention, for example, of any boys or apprentices whose presence was not uncommon at this period. Perhaps there were none; who knows? It seems clear enough that there were stringed instruments and professional musicians to play them, and that some of them were good singers. It seems also that the household acquired an organ (Fig 3), perhaps at the same time as the minstrels' gallery was erected in the great hall; but whether it was originally used in the chapel is another question.[56]

However, standards of hospitality were declining at this period, and fewer servants were retained.[57] Moreover, the Sackville fortunes were diminishing. The 2nd Earl, who survived his father only by a year, is said to have been 'wildly extravagant', and

3 The organ now in the chapel at Knole. Bought by the 1st Earl of Dorset, between about 1605 and 1608

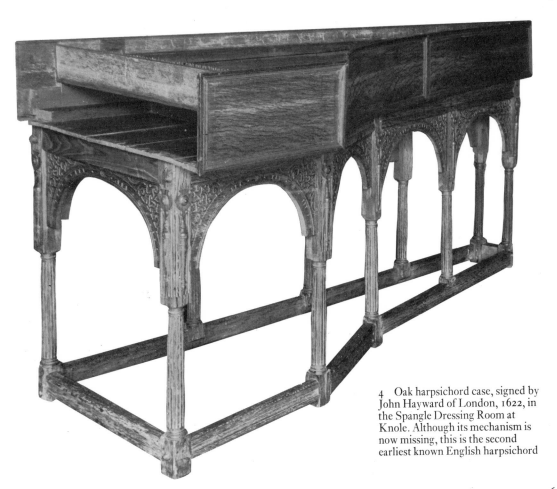

4 Oak harpsichord case, signed by John Hayward of London, 1622, in the Spangle Dressing Room at Knole. Although its mechanism is now missing, this is the second earliest known English harpsichord

his directions for his funeral suggest that he had not inherited his father's streak of melancholy.[58] This impoverishment of the estate continued under the 3rd Earl: a letter of his to the Council in 1620 mentions his 'weak estate' and many debts, which amounted to £60,000 at his death in 1624, commemorated by Henry Peacham, the author of *The Compleat Gentleman* two years earlier.[59] Anne Clifford, his wife, had received some musical education, and possessed a considerable fortune of her own; unfortunately, however, she disliked Knole, as the diarist John Evelyn was to do years later.[60] Gone were the days when Knole boasted professional musicians in its midst, although there may very possibly have been quite adequate performers in the household. A harpsichord case now in the Spangle dressing room (Fig 4) is signed John Hayward of London and dated 1622, which makes it the second earliest instrument of this type in England. But it is uncertain whether it was acquired by the 3rd Earl of Dorset and his wife, or whether it belonged to the Cranfield family and was brought from Copt Hall to Knole later in the seventeenth century.[61]

During the Civil War Knole was entered by the Parliamentary forces, and the Sackvilles lost possession of the house in 1643-44.[62] The family interest in music and the arts, however, survived this deprivation. Charles, who succeeded as 6th Earl in 1677, was a not inconsiderable poet.[63] Of particular interest to our present purpose is his ballad, 'To all ye ladies now at land', which was probably known to Pepys.[64] This

5 *Thomas D'Urfey* (1653–1723) by John van der Gucht. Canvas, 71.7 by 60.6 cm. A playwright, poet and ballad-monger, D'Urfey was an intimate friend of the 6th Earl of Dorset, and for a time librarian at Knole

6 'Madame Muscovita' (Lucia Panichi) by Rosalba Carriera. Pastel, 54.3 by 47.5 cm. An Italian opera singer, who became mistress of the 1st Duke of Dorset's eldest son, Lord Middlesex, in the 1740s

was included in the 1714 and 1720 editions of *Wit and Mirth, or Pills to purge Melancholy*. This was a collection of ballads and songs with which was associated Thomas D'Urfey, a popular dramatist and versifier, whose burial in 1723 was paid for by Lord Dorset's son, the 1st Duke. D'Urfey's portrait (Fig 5) is still to be found at Knole, where he is thought to have been librarian for a time.[65] Other verses by the 6th Earl are included in other song-collections, and Purcell set two of his songs as incidental music for comedies by Thomas Southerne.[66] A score of Purcell's *Indian Queen* is still at Knole.

None of the 1st Duke's three sons achieved any notable distinction.[67] The eldest, Lord Middlesex, went on the Grand Tour and subsequently succeeded in losing money in promoting concerts and Italian opera in London. He wrote bad verses to his mistress, 'Madame Muscovita', a singer named Lucia Panichi (Fig 6), whose abilities did not commend themselves to everyone, despite her popularity in the early 1740s.[68] It is only fair to point out that the Duke did not approve of his son's profligacy, but his protests seem to have been ignored.[69] Not that His Grace was unmusical: he attended performances of Handel's works in Dublin in 1751 and 1753, during his term as Lord Lieutenant.[70]

It is during the latter half of the century, however, that we gain the clearest picture of the richness of musical life at Knole.[71] John Frederick, the 3rd Duke, was at the centre of a musical circle in Rome when Dr Charles Burney visited there in 1770, and in the 1780s served as British ambassador in Paris.[72] Hardly surprisingly, the Duke had a wide musical interest, shown by an undated music catalogue still at Knole. This

7   The plaster cast of the dancer, Giannetta Baccelli, mistress of the 3rd Duke of Dorset, at the foot of the Great Stairs, Knole

8 *Madame Baccelli posing to Gainsborough*, detail of a drawing by an anonymous artist (possibly Ozias Humphrey) *c* 1782. Pencil and black ink on canvas, 87.6 by 120.6 cm. The scene takes place in the Ballroom at Knole, with Wang-y-Tong, the 3rd Duke's Chinese servant, in the background. Gainsborough's portrait, exhibited at the Royal Academy in 1782, was recently acquired by the Tate Gallery

account is manifestly incomplete: at one place the compiler wearied of his task, and wrote laconically '&c., &c., &c.' at the end of one of the lengthier sections to indicate that not all the music in that section had been listed. Elsewhere, however, additions were made subsequently in another hand. Even so, there is music still at Knole that is not entered, such as the scores of Handel's *Acis and Galatea*, to be dated between 1785 and 1803, and *Jephtha* (1768–76), and a verse anthem by James Kent, *Hear my Prayer* (1783–89).

Two other items omitted from the catalogues are perhaps more significant. The 3rd Duke followed the example of his predecessor in patronising London opera – though less disastrously; his accounts show frequent subscriptions in 1768–69 and again at the end of his life in 1790 and 1796–99; we may assume that if our records had been fuller we would find that payments continued regularly over the whole period, for at the end of 1776 Rauzzini produced at the King's Theatre in the Haymarket his opera *Le Ali d'Amore* which he had dedicated to the Duke. At that time one of the dancers that gave pleasure to the patrons was Giannetta Baccelli (Figs 7 and 8). With her the Duke was infatuated; he established her at Knole with her own entourage, in what is still known as 'Shelley's Tower' (after the servants' corruption of her name), and did not part from her until shortly before his marriage in 1790.[73] Thus there are at Knole two collections of *The Celebrated (Opera) Dances*, composed by G. B. Noferi (1781) and Borghi and others (1783), with which Baccelli's name is associated (Fig 9). None of these works, however, appears in the catalogue, unless the opera masquerades under the title *The Agreeable Surprize*, which is otherwise unexplained.

Curiously enough, opera and vocal music appears little in the catalogue. The brief section devoted to vocal music lists a few operas: besides Philidor's *Carmen Seculare*, a 'flattering success' when it came out in 1779, there are *Leucippo*, with which Matteo Vento introduced himself at the King's Theatre in 1764,[74] Sacchini's *Oedipe à Colone*

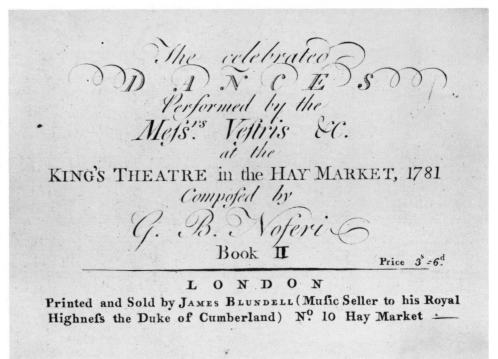

9 The title page of G. B. Noferi's *The Celebrated Dances performed at the King's Theatre in the Hay Market*, 1781, in the library at Knole. The names of the dancers include 'Signora Bacchelli'

(Versailles, 1786) – apparently a favourite, for there is a collection of 'traversa [flute] airs' separately listed – as well as selections from Rauzzini's *Piramo e Tisbe* (King's Theatre, 1775), *The Quaker*, perhaps *La Quakera Spiritosa* (Naples, 1783), by Guglielmi (the Duke had paid for the copying of a rondo and a song by him in 1777[75]) and Bianchi's *Les Sabots*. Otherwise there is nothing, apart from '*Varietés à la Mode*, 1-3', perhaps an entry for the undated *A Choice Collection of the Most Favorite French Songs sung at the Comédie Italienne at Paris*, and six books of catches; the accounts record a payment of six guineas in March 1769 to the Catch Club, which had held meetings since 1761/62.[76]

The main interest of the catalogue lies in the wealth of instrumental music it records, both chamber and orchestral. There are, however, difficulties in interpreting it. We have noticed that it does not seem to be a complete record of the music in the house; items noted in the accounts are not recorded in the catalogue. Moreover, details given are often not full enough for music to be identified, and occasionally they are misleading: Phillipp Meyer's *Twelve English Songs*, for example, is listed as vocal music, although the title clearly indicates that these are instrumental pieces.[77] It is clear that there is some duplication of entries; what is not clear is how extensive that duplication may be.

It is quite evident, however, that the Duke possessed a very extensive library of music, chiefly for small ensembles (duos, trios and quartets) with some works designated as solos (with thoroughbass accompaniment) and keyboard sonatas. A quantity of this music is entered anonymously, but nevertheless eighty-seven composers are named, additional to others named in the accounts. Some of the music the 3rd Duke perhaps inherited; Corelli's *concerti grossi* of 1714 and some sonatas are the earliest pieces listed, although there are also pieces by Tartini and a concerto by Barsanti. The fact that the Duke bought a portrait of Corelli, said to be by Tito Maio (Fig 10), from Reynolds in 1776, suggests however that he may have bought Corelli's music himself. One might have expected to find Geminiani, Handel or perhaps Arne represented by some instrumental music; but the collection is almost entirely devoted to composers active

10 *Arcangelo Corelli* (1653–1733). Canvas, 60.9 by 73.7 cm (Collection: Lord Sackville). The portrait was bought by the 3rd Duke of Dorset from Sir Joshua Reynolds in 1776 as by 'Tito Maio'. Corelli's *concerti grossi* of 1714 and some of his sonatas are among the earliest pieces listed in the Duke's library of music

11 *Felice Giardini* (1716–96) by Thomas Gainsborough, bought by the 3rd Duke of Dorset in 1763. Canvas 74.3 by 61.6 cm. The composer who was most closely associated with the Duke's music-making at Knole

in the latter half of the century when native English composers produced only inferior instrumental music. So we find that pride of place is given to such men as Abel, J. C. Bach, Giardini (whose portrait (Fig 11) is at Knole), Pleyel, Boccherini and Haydn. We may suspect that Giardini's was a strong influence in shaping the Duke's musical taste. He seems to have been a frequent visitor to the house: the records show substantial payments to him in 1785 and 1790, and probably others were recorded in papers now missing. A number of these other composers may well have been Giardini's associates. For long he was involved with the King's Theatre, and the formative influences on the collection seem to centre on this institution, and to a lesser extent on the rest of London's musical life.

The collection was indeed a curious one. A number of the composers represented seem otherwise to be unknown, and at least one may have been in the Duke's service. The French violinist Pierre Vachon, who is noted in London during 1772, contributed a set of six duos and many quartets and divertimenti[78] to the Duke's music library. Is he to be identified with the Mr Vachon who settled a number of the Duke's bills in the mid-1770s?[79] Another possible servant is the mysterious Mümler. He wrote (or perhaps merely possessed) a song that was printed at the Duke's expense in 1798, and the accounts record various payments to him, culminating in his salary to Michaelmas the following year.[80] The same may be said for Bernard Rivers, the only name in the catalogue to be distinguished by a Christian name, and Witton, who had written solos and duos respectively, although the only other British representative in the list, Blake, was a member of the Royal band.

Other minor figures are well represented. Antonin Kammel is one of the most frequent names; he made his debut as a violinist at one of J. C. Bach's concerts in May 1768, having been a pupil of Tartini.[81] Another is that of the baryton player Lidel, whose playing excited Burney's admiration.[82] The violinist Noferi, whom we have already met as composer of dances for Baccelli and others, was represented also by two sets of trios, one of which was bought in 1781 from James Blundell, a music seller near the King's Theatre in the Haymarket. 'Noferi the Musick Master' had received £8 5s od in 1767 from the 3rd Duke, before his succession;[83] but only Cervetto and Lanzetti of those who were writing in a similar style at that period were included – even Gluck was overlooked.[84] Similarly, the now-forgotten opera composer Misliwecek contributed a quartet and a number of trios; but Mozart is omitted, although he had spent some time in London and the other had not.[85]

It seems clear that this library had been accumulated by the 3rd Duke almost alone, although probably he had inherited a few items. We have suggested that the violinist Giardini influenced its selection, and that the King's Theatre itself played a part. The amounts subscribed by the Duke suggest that he paid frequent visits, and doubtless he would have developed an affinity for musicians he had come to know there. Consequently it comes as no surprise to find that composers and executants connected with the theatre found favour with the Duke (we recall Baccelli), and that their compositions found the way into his library. This explains the presence of the works of Kammel as well as those of the violinist Barthélémon, the oboist Le Brun and the cellist Giordani, as well as Bianchi (who directed there as early as 1780[86]), Corri,[87] Saccini and of course Rauzzini, to name those better represented.

But this alone is not sufficient as an explanation; not all the composers even visited London or had operas given there. There were indeed subscription concerts, and the accounts show that the family patronised such events early in the last century, after the 3rd Duke's death. There were, for example, subscriptions in 1802 to 'the Ancient Music' and 'the Vocal Concert', and doubtless other such enterprises received the family's support.[88] There was formerly in the house the portrait of a singer named Sarah Bates. She was the wife of Joah Bates, who directed the concerts of Ancient Music until 1793. We thus have reason to suppose that the 3rd Duke also patronised public concerts, thereby enlarging his musical knowledge. In addition to Haydn's, he may have come into contact with the works of Raimondi, Pleyel and Schwindl by this means, although Schwindl, according to Burney,[89] fell out of favour after Giardini's departure in 1784. This suggests that Giardini may have introduced Schwindl's music to the Duke.

There is another point worth noticing, however. A glance at the publishers represented in the collection suggests that they were all within a short distance of the theatre. John Welcker and James Blundell, whose bills survive, were in the Haymarket; and Longman & Broderip, who published Barthélémon, had a shop there at the end of 1782. The Duke also had dealings (through Vachon) with William Napier, who had his shop in the Strand near Charing Cross; at the other end of the Strand, opposite Somerset House, was to be found Robert Bremner between 1762 and 1789; his music was prominent in the Duke's collection. At the same period (1776) the Duke had a 'tenor' (viola) repaired by J. & G. Vogler, and hired a second instrument from them; their premises were in Glasshouse Street, which runs from the north-west corner of Piccadilly Circus, to the north of the Haymarket. To the east, running north from Trafalgar Square, lies St Martin's Lane, where William Forster published Cambini about 1780; five years later he moved to the Strand. At the eastern end of that street, Catherine Street runs north from the Aldwych, near Somerset House; here were to be found at this period William Randall, publisher of the Knole score of Handel's *Jephtha*, from 1768 to about 1776, and a little later (1785) onwards H. Wright, who put out *Acis*.[90] Perhaps the Duke or his agent, Vachon, bought music at sight at one or other of these establishments. James Kent's publishers, Birchall & Andrews, were a little more distant from the Haymarket in New Bond Street.[91]

All this, however, is supposition. We are on surer ground when we consider the instrumental resources the Duke needed, though indeed the evidence is none too plentiful. No doubt the slender resources on hand at the house were responsible for the neglect of opera. The Duke himself seems to have been devoted to the house, and to have held concerts in the Cartoon Gallery.[92] Perhaps he himself, like Frederick the Great and Lord Abingdon, played the flute: the instrument had the distinction of a section in the catalogue headed 'Traversa', listing eight duos in manuscript and twelve quartets, as well as the airs from *Oedipe* we have already mentioned; but we have no means of telling whether this list includes the six quartets listed elsewhere, Bach's six quartets, op 8, for German (or transverse) flute, violin, tenor (viola) and 'cello, or the set written jointly by Bach, Abel and Giardini for a similar combination.[93] There were also some solos by Bianchi, and others for violin and 'cello, as well as harpsichord pieces. These latter presumably were kept for Giardini, Kammel, Cervetto and perhaps other visiting musicians from London; Kammel's solos and duets are particularly well represented, and a set of 'cello solos by Cervetto (presumably those with a thoroughbass accompaniment published *c* 1740–55). Giardini also contributed solo pieces; but most of his were for tenor (viola), an instrument that Kammel played,[94]

12   The bay window in the Cartoon Gallery, showing a Kirkman harpsichord,
of c 1770, and a mahogany violin case. The Duke regularly held concerts in the
Cartoon Gallery when at Knole

13 Detail of the crest and cypher of the 3rd Duke of Dorset, on the lid of the violin case in Fig 12

as were two of his concertos.[95] Twelve of his *duetti per violino e viola*, inscribed 'per il Duca Dorsset', are in the British Library; they are not shown in the Knole catalogue.[96]

Towards the end of his life the Duke became temperamentally unstable, and his interest in opera gradually declined. As early as 1782, even before Giardini's departure, we find a bill for ten weeks' hire of a pianoforte, an early specimen from Christopher Ganer, and the Cartoon Gallery still houses a Kirkman harpsichord of *c* 1770 as well as a violin case bearing the Duke's crest (Fig 12).[97] His Duchess, whom he married in 1790, was evidently not unsympathetic to music, although she was austere enough to forbid conversation during meals.[98] It was she who settled accounts for hire of harpsichords and a grand pianoforte from John Broadwood between the time of her marriage in 1790 and 1792; there is still at Knole a manuscript book of short-score exercises 'della Duchessa Dorsset' dated 1793, and one Martini wrote piano pieces dedicated to her.

Payments for music – an organ, dancing and tambourine lessons for the children, even payments for the opera – continued in 1798–99; in 1801–2 appear subscriptions to concerts and the Sevenoaks ball, and a payment 'for an opera box for one night' – the days of lavish subscriptions had passed finally with the Duke.[99] But clearly the musical interests of the children were encouraged by their mother: one of them was presented with a manuscript of some of Bianchi's music by 'the most wretched of mothers' in 1807, and the girls had pieces written for them: a *duettino* the same year,

175

and the next an *arietta* for Lady Mary, the elder. There are also Agrippino Rosselli's duets; these are undated, but they must antedate Mary's marriage to the Earl of Plymouth in August 1811.

Her younger sister, Elizabeth, who married the 5th Earl de la Warr, inherited Knole after her death in 1864.[100] Musicmaking continued in the house in their day, and our last glimpse of music at Knole is of the programme of a concert of vocal music on 11 June 1853. It was given by amateurs, with nine items in the first part and eleven in the second, and concluded with a 'grand chorus by the whole company'.

Notes

1 Frank W. Jessup, *A History of Kent* (1974), p 68; F. R. H. Du Boulay, *The Lordship of Canterbury* (1966), p 195; V. Sackville-West, *Knole and the Sackvilles* 4th edn (1958), p 21.

2 Edward Carpenter, *Cantuar* (1971), p 76.

3 His will gives practically no reference to it (*Archaeologia Cantiana*, XXIV (1900), pp 244-52); but that of course proves nothing.

4 Du Boulay, p 238; Irene Josephine Churchill, *Canterbury Administration* (1933), vol 1, pp 191n, 192, 193, 405, 406 & n; vol 2, p 139.

5 See Frank Ll. Harrison, *Music in Medieval Britain* (London, 1958), pp 24-5, and note the provision made by Bishop Foxe for musicians' seats at Durham Castle at this period (L. F. Salzman, *Building in England down to 1540* (Oxford, 1967), p 410). On the chapel, see Sackville-West, pp 31-2. For Henry VII, see L. Sackville-West, *Knole House* (Sevenoaks, 1906), pp 2-3.

6 Carpenter, p 82. Among his guests may well have been the young King Henry VIII, who seems to have visited the house more than once in 1515-16 (Edward Hasted, *History and Topographical Survey of the County of Kent*, vol 3 (Canterbury, 1797), p 65).

7 *Letters and Papers, Henry VIII*, vol 13, Pt 1 (1892), no. 195.

8 Du Boulay, p 324. See L. Baldwin Smith, *Henry VIII: the Mask of Royalty* (1971), p 232; J. J. Scarisbrick, *Henry VIII* (1968), pp 17, 485-86.

9 Public Record Office, E 101/422/13.

10 *Letters and Papers*, vol 16 (1898), p 324.

11 Scarisbrick, pp 15-16. See also the extract from Henry Peacham (1634) in *Source Readings in Music History*, ed Oliver Strunk (New York, 1950), p 333.

12 See the quotation from Edward Hall's *Chronicle* (STC 12720-23) in Percy M. Young, *A History of British Music* (1967), p 89, and *The Autobiography of Thomas Whythorne*, ed James M. Osborn (Oxford, 1961), p 232. Doubtless this account is highly coloured, but it indicates at least the kind of tradition that became current.

13 Scarisbrick, pp 484-86, 426-27; Smith, pp 233-34. Note the presence by the king's deathbed of his flautist Patrec (*ibid*, pp 13, 19).

14 Young, p 90; Harrison, pp 171-72; *The King's Musick*, ed Henry Cart de Lafontaine (1909), p 5.

15 *Calendar of Patent Rolls, Philip and Mary*, vol 3 (1938), p 71.

16 Philip Hughes, *The Reformation of England*, 5th edn (1963), vol 2, p 185.

17 *Calendar of Patent Rolls, Elizabeth I*, vol 2 (1948), pp 190, 191; John Buxton, *Elizabethan Taste* (1965), p 47; Ian Dunlop, *Palaces and Progresses of Elizabeth I* (1962), p 43.

18 Walter L. Woodfill, *Musicians in English Society* (Princeton, 1953), pp 63, 65; Young, p 108.

19 PRO, E 101/431/4.

20 *King's Musick*, pp 23-24.

21 Buxton, pp 172-73; J. E. Neale, *Queen Elizabeth I* (1960), pp 22, 131.

22 As is stated by William Durrant Cooper (*Sussex Archaeological Collections*, V (1852), p 191) and A. L. Rowse (*The Elizabethan Renaissance: the Life of the Society* (1971), p 93).

23 A. L. Rowse, *The Elizabethan Renaissance: the Cultural Achievement* (1972), pp 111-12 (Worcester's remarks are quoted also in E. H. Fellowes, *William Byrd*, 2nd edn (Oxford, 1948), p 157, where Byrd's song is identified); Neale, pp 216, 323. See also Smith, pp 80-82, and John Stevens, *Music and Poetry in the Early Tudor Court* (1961), pp 244-46 and chap 12, with Buxton, pp 173-74.

24 Vol cit, pp 70, 103. Neale comments (p 212) that there was need only to surrender a house to the Queen's use.

25 *Calendar of State Papers, Domestic*, vol 1 (1547-80) (1856), p 322; *Cal. Pat. Rolls, Eliz. I*, vol 5 (1966), no. 1894, and vol 2, p 438.

26 Fellowes, pp 14-16.

27 Apparently on rather flimsy grounds, by Thurston Dart in *Music and Letters*, XLV (1964), p 21; see Alan Brown in *Proceedings of the Royal Musical Association*, XCV (1969), pp 29-30.

28 Hasted, p 69; *DNB*; *Cal. Pat. Rolls, Eliz. I*, vol 5, no. 1953.

29 Fellowes, p 151. But H. S. Bennett has pointed out (*English Books and Readers, 1558 to 1603* (Cambridge, 1965), pp 37-39) the political nature of such dedications.

30 Fellowes, *English Madrigal Composers*, 2nd edn (Oxford, 1948), p 80; Rowse, *Cultural Achievement* p 117. For the piece, see *The Collected Lute Music of John Dowland*, ed Diana Poulton and Basil Lam (1974), p 126.

31 *DNB*. For extracts from the Althorp household accounts, see Woodfill, pp 273-74.

32 The identification accepted by Hughes-Hughes (*Catalogue of Manuscript Music in the British Museum*, vol 3 (1909), p 481). See *Collected Lute Music*, p 178, and Diana Poulton, *John Dowland* (1972).

33 Hasted, p 69.

34 Ibid, p 70; V. Sackville-West, p 50.

35 *STC*, nos. 18684-85 (see V. de Sola Pinto, *The English Renaissance, 1510-1688*, 3rd edn (1966), p 225); Buxton, p 215. According to F. W. Sternfeld (*Music in Shakespearean Tragedy* (1963), pp 214-15), *Gorboduc* was 'the earliest English tragedy to employ both blank verse and dumb-show with instrumental music'; see also *ibid*, pp 216-17.

36 Woodfill, p 63; *Grove's Dictionary of Music and Musicians*, 5th edn (1954), s.v. Daman. On his works, see Ernst H. Meyer, *English Chamber Music* (1946), pp 94-95; *Historical Companion to Hymns Ancient and Modern*, ed Maurice Frost (1962), pp 54-55, and Frost, *English and Scottish Psalm and Hymn Tunes* (1953), pp 21-24.

37 V. Sackville-West, pp 49-50; Susi Jeans in *Monthly Musical Record*, LXXXVIII (1958), p 183.

38 Jeans, 'Seventeenth-Century Musicians in the Sackville Papers', loc cit, pp 182-87; and East Sussex Record Office MS De La Warr 592 (an indenture establishing the trust for the Society of Musicians, 28 August 1739).

39 V. Sackville-West, p 50.

40 Eric Mercer, *English Art, 1553-1625* (1962), p 121.

41 Kent Archives Office, U269 A1/1 (given by Jeans, pp 182-83).

42 *King's Musick*, p 50.

43 *The Old Cheque-book*, ed Edward F. Rimbault (Camden Society, 1872), pp 204, 99-100, 57.

44 Woodfill, pp 301-3; cf *Grove's Dictionary*, s.v. He may well have been related to Peter Lupo.

45 *King's Musick*, p 57.

46 Ibid, pp 59, 61-63, 125, 150.

47 Jeans, p 183.

48 J. and J. A. Venn, *Alumni Cantabrigenses* (Cambridge, 1927) and Joseph Foster, *Alumni Oxonienses, 1500-1714* (Oxford, 1890-92), s.vv.

49 Mercer, pp 160, 162; the portrait is no. 234 in the Knole collection.

50 Listed in *Grove's Dictionary*, s.v.

51 Ernst H. Meyer, *English Chamber Music* (1946), p 179.

52 Brit. Lib. MSS Add. 29372-7; cf MS Add. 29427.

53 Venn (op cit, part 1, vol 4, p 76 ii) notes a William Symmes who held benefices in Kent after 1587. The name occurs in two PCC wills of 1644/5 (PRO Prob. 11/192, folio 331a) and 1650, relating to East Farleigh; but there are no references to music.

54 Rowse, *Cultural Achievements*, p 130; Woodfill, pp 233-34 (note the comment about regular engagement on p 65); Young, pp 127-28; Gladys Scott Thomson, *Life in a Noble Household, 1641-1700* (1940), p 65.

55 *King's Musick*, p 45.

56 Woodfill, pp 68-70; David Cecil, *The Cecils of Hatfield House* (1975), p 146. The organ is shown as being in 'the Organ Room' in two inventories of 1765 and 1799 (Kent AO MSS. U269 E4; E5, p 46);

it was still there in 1906 (L. Sackville-West, p 50), together with a spinet dated *c* 1610. There is also at the house a harpsichord case dated 1622.

57 Woodfill, pp 67-68; Lawrence Stone, *The Crisis of the Aristocracy, 1558-1641*, abridged edn (Oxford 1967), p 266; Christopher Hill, *Society and Puritanism in Pre-Revolutionary England* (1966), p 279; Dunlop, pp 122-23 (cf p 179).

58 Rowse, *The England of Elizabeth* (1950), p 317; Stone, p 263.

59 *Cal. SP Dom James I 1619-1623* (1858), p 198; Stone, p 246; V. Sackville-West, p 81. For a commemorative effusion by Henry Peacham (above, n 11), see *STC*, no. 19499.

60 V. Sackville-West, pp 63, 67; Buxton, p 81; Evelyn described it as 'a greate old fashioned house' in 1673 (*Diary*, ed E. S. de Beer (Oxford, 1959), p 589).

61 For the household musicians, see the seating arrangements in 1613-24 (V. Sackville-West, pp 85-88); for the harpsichord see Donald H. Boalch, *Makers of the Harpsichord and Clavichord, 1440 to 1840* (1956), p 48.

62 Ibid, pp 104-8; Jessup, p 105.

63 de Sola Pinto, pp 352-53; V. Sackville-West, pp 147-50.

64 Ibid, pp 122-23. Pepys's allusion (2 January 1664/65) is not unequivocal.

65 Cyrus Lawrence Day and Eleanore Boswell Murrie, *English Song-Books, 1651-1702: a Bibliography* (Bibliographical Society, 1940), nos 228, 242; *DNB*. See also John Hawkins, *A General History of the Science and Practice of Music* (1853; reprinted 1963), vol 2, pp 818-19; for the portrait see catalogue no. 167.

66 Day and Murrie, nos 1574, 1791; Franklin B. Zimmerman, *Henry Purcell, 1659-1695: an Analytical Catalogue of his Music* (1963), nos 588(4), 612(1).

67 V. Sackville-West, pp 153-54.

68 Ibid, p 169; Otto Erich Deutsch, *Handel: a Documentary Biography* (1955), pp 477, 524, 528, 541, 567; Charles Burney, *A General History of Music*, ed Frank Mercer (1935), vol 2, pp 827, 850.

69 Charles J. Phillips, *History of the Sackville Family* (1929), vol 2, pp 85-86. See also Burney and Deutsch.

70 Deutsch, pp 713, 745. It is interesting to note that Handel paid three visits to Tunbridge Wells (ibid, pp 369, 394, 622, 806-7; see below, n 85). A portrait at Knole (catalogue no. 206) by Balthasar Denner is traditionally thought to represent Handel, though recent research suggests that it is not a likeness of the composer.

71 For much information, particularly from the household accounts, I am deeply indebted to Mr John Harvey.

72 V. Sackville-West, pp 178-82.

73 Ibid, pp 182-85; Charles Sanford Terry, *John Christian Bach: a Biography* (Oxford, 1929), pp 150n, 163n.

74 Terry, p 77.

75 Shown in the accounts (Kent AO U269 A243/7), but not in the catalogue (see below).

76 On the club see Burney, vol cit, p 1022. In the library at Knole there is a set of Thomas Evans's collection of words of *Old Ballads* (1784).

77 British Library, Reference Division, A 868 1(4).

78 This variety of nomenclature is of no significance to our present purpose; see Ruth Halle Rowen, *Early Chamber Music* (1949), pp 140-45; cf Egon Wellesz and Frederick Sternfeld (eds), *The Age of Enlightenment, 1745-1790* (Oxford, 1973), pp 503-7.

79 Kent AO U269 A243/8. Note the remarks of F. M. L. Thompson on the dependence of the landed aristocrat on his servants at this period (*English Landed Society in the Nineteenth Century* (1963), pp 95-96).

80 U269 A4/1-4. Another item not in the catalogue.

81 Terry, p 115.

82 Vol cit, p 1020.

83 U269 A12.

84 As discussed by William S. Newman in *The Sonata in the Baroque Era* (North Carolina, 1959), pp 327-38. On Cervetto, see Terry, pp 156-58.

85 See *The Letters of Mozart and his Family*, ed Emily Anderson (1938), vol 1, pp 64-83. On p 71 Leopold Mozart mentions a proposed visit to Tunbridge [Wells] at the beginning of July 1764.

86 Terry, p 163. A list of London orchestral musicians over this period is in Adam Carse, *The Orchestra in the XVIIIth Century* (1940), pp 79-80.

87 Terry, p 148.

88 On London concerts at this period, see Ernest Walker, *A History of Music in England*, ed J. A. Westrup (Oxford, 1952), pp 273-74; also Terry, pp 63-64, and Carse, pp 76-82. On the 'Ancient Music', see Burney, vol cit, p 1022, and the quotation from Samuel Wesley in Young, *History of British Music*, p 384.

89 Vol cit, pp 957-58. A performance of a Schwindl symphony in 1779-80 is mentioned by Young (p 389n.). See also Wellesz and Sternfeld, p 429.

90 For details of these publishers, see Charles Humphries and William C. Smith, *Music Publishing in the British Isles* (1954, with corrigenda attached to reissue 1970). There are also account entries in 1769 for Covent Garden and Drury Lane theatres (U269 A12).

91 The Duke had also a considerable amount of music copied in 1776-77 (U269 A243/6-7), and probably at other times.

92 L. Sackville-West, pp 68-69; compare V. Sackville-West, p 186.

93 Terry, pp 306-7, 309. It should be explained that the catalogue is arranged in two parts: the first is evidently an inventory, arranged alphabetically according to the letters designating the places in which the music was kept; the second is a rough classification by genre, and includes some composers, presumably those most in demand. The difficulty lies in establishing the relation between the two, for the second includes music not represented in the first.

94 Carse, p 80.

95 See Rowan, p 147.

96 MSS. Add. 31695-6 (*Catalogue of Manuscript Music*, vol 3, p 180).

97 U269 A243/12; Boalch, p 33. For the harpsichord, *ibid*, p 66, no. 99.

98 L. Sackville-West, p 59; V. Sackville-West, p 190.

99 U269 A252. The hire and tuning of harpsichords and pianofortes continue to appear in the accounts until 1820, and in 1804 there was an item for the repair of violins (A252/11, 12, 15, 21-22, 31).

100 V. Sackville-West, p 210; *Burke's Peerage*, 105th edn (1970), pp 2333-34.

Acknowledgment

I am grateful to Mr and Mrs Hugh Sackville-West for their help and hospitality at Knole.

Notes on Contributors

Roger Alma lectures in English at Worcester College of Higher Education, where he is Director of Studies for the BA degree. He has a particular interest in the relationship between poetry, painting and landscape gardening in the eighteenth century, and in subsequent changing perceptions of the natural world and man's relation to it.

Dr Charles Avery is Deputy Keeper of the Department of Architecture & Sculpture at the Victoria & Albert Museum. He is an authority on Italian Renaissance and Northern Mannerist sculpture, with a special interest in English sculpture during the reign of King Charles I. He is currently working on a *catalogue raisonné* of the work of Hubert Le Sueur for the Walpole Society.

Major David Back, formerly a serving officer in the Royal Artillery, is the author of books dealing with gunmakers working in the eighteenth and nineteenth centuries and the arms they made. Apart from his writing, he restores a wide variety of antiques.

Geoffrey Beard is Director of the Visual Arts Centre in the University of Lancaster. He is the author of books on *Georgian Craftsmen*, *Decorative Plasterwork in Great Britain*, and *The Work of Robert Adam*.

John Cornforth is a regular contributor to *Country Life*, and was architectural editor of the magazine from 1966 to 1978. He is on the Historic Buildings Council, a member of the Properties Committee and the Art and Architectural Panels of the National Trust, and author (with the late John Fowler) of *English Decoration in the 18th Century*, published in 1974.

Dudley Dodd is Historic Buildings Representative for the National Trust in Wessex, and author of guide books to several houses in the region, including those for Montacute House, Dunster Castle and Mompesson House, Salisbury.

Wyn K. Ford is an editor with an interest in archives. He has written on both local history and English music; he was a contributor to the supplementary volume of *Grove's Dictionary of Music*, and the compiler of *Music in England before 1800: a Select Bibliography*.

Terence Hodgkinson has been Director of the Wallace Collection since 1974, and was previously Keeper of the Department of Architecture and Sculpture at the Victoria & Albert Museum. His *Catalogue of Sculpture at Waddesdon* and *Catalogue of Sculpture in the Frick Collection*, New York, were both published in 1970.

Pierre de la Ruffinière du Prey teaches architectural history in the Department of Art, Queen's University, Kingston, Ontario, Canada. He has made a special study of the early career of Sir John Soane, and is currently writing a book on the subject.

Francis Russell is a member of the Drawings Department at Christie's, and has contributed articles on art historical subjects to a number of learned journals. He is preparing books on painters of the Umbrian School, and on Pompeo Batoni.

John Sales succeeded Graham Thomas in 1974 as the National Trust's Gardens Adviser with overall responsibility for properties throughout England and Wales. He is the author of a number of articles in *Garden History*, the *Journal of the Royal Horticultural Society* and other periodicals, and is also editor of the Batsford series, *Gardens of Britain*.

Edward Saunders is an architect and an occasional architectural historian. His chief interest lies in the study of the antique and the restoration of old buildings. He is at present engaged in research for a book on the work of Jean Tijou and the English wrought iron smiths of the eighteenth century.

Henry Summerson catalogued the Charlecote Library for the National Trust in 1976, after successfully submitting a thesis on medieval crime for a doctorate at Cambridge.

Philip Watson is currently completing an honours degree in Ecology at the New University of Ulster. Formerly employed in sea-fisheries research with the Northern Ireland Department of Agriculture, and one time regional officer in the province for the Royal Society for the Protection of Birds, he has recently been researching on sea-birds in Canada and around Ireland's north coast.

Acknowledgments

The illustrations to articles which are not credited below are the copyright of the National Trust.

Thomas Hardy and Stourhead
by Roger Alma
1, 4, 12 Dorset County Museum
2, 8, 10, 11, 13-15 John Bethell
3 National Portrait Gallery
5, 6 Author

Hubert le Sueur's Bronze Portraits of King Charles I
by Charles Avery
1 British Museum (reproduced by kind permission of the Trustees)
2, 6-10, 12, 20-22, 24 Victoria and Albert Museum
3 Bodleian Library, Oxford
4 Musée Jacquemart-André (Photographie Bulloz)
5, 11, 14, 23 Author
9 Department of the Environment
13 Courtauld Institute of Art
15-17 O. G. Jarman
18 Department of the Environment
19 Musée de Dijon
22, 23 Sotheby & Co.

Firearms at Felbrigg
by D. H. L. Back
1-12 National Trust (GGS Photography, Norwich)

Edward Goudge: 'The Beste Master in England'
by Geoffrey Beard
1, 3, 4 Country Life Ltd
2 Bodleian Library, Oxford
5, 6 R.I.B.A. Drawings Collection
7-9 National Trust

John Fowler and the National Trust
by John Cornforth
1 Gervase Jackson-Stops
2 Aerofilms
3, 6, 9, 10 Country Life Ltd
4, 5, 8 Jeremy Whitaker
7 Angelo Hornak

Rebuilding Stourhead, 1902-1906
by Dudley Dodd
4, 9-11, 14, 16 Angelo Hornak
6 John Harris (by kind permission of Mr Paul Mellon)
7 National Portrait Gallery
8 Jeremy Whitaker
13 Edwin Smith

Music at Knole
by Wyn K. Ford
1 Country Life Ltd
2 National Monuments Record
3, 9, 12, 13 John Bethell
4 Geo. P. King
5-8, 10, 11 Courtauld Institute of Art

Companions of Diana at Cliveden
by Terence Hodgkinson
1 Israel Museum, Jerusalem
2 National Gallery of Art, Washington
3-6 Raymond Thatcher
7, 8 Musée du Louvre (Cabinet des Estampes)

John Soane, Philip Yorke and their Quest for Primitive Architecture
by Pierre de la Ruffiniere du Prey
1, 6, 9, 10 Sir John Soane Museum
4 Victoria and Albert Museum
7 Vassar College Art Gallery (Peter A. Juley & Son)
11-13 Gervase Jackson-Stops

The British Portraits of Anton Raphael Mengs
by Francis Russell
1 Prudence Cumming Associates Ltd
2 Royal Academy of Arts
3 Anderson & McMeekin Photography
4-6 Courtauld Institute of Art

**High Victorian Horticulture: the Garden
at Waddesdon**
by John Sales
1-3 National Trust
4, 9-11 John Bethell
5-8, 12-15 Author (copies of stereoscopic transparencies
by kind permission of Mrs James de Rothschild)

**'Mr Warren' and the Wrought Iron Gates at
Clandon and Powis**
by Edward Saunders
1-4, 8, 10 Country Life Ltd
5 Jeremy Whitaker
6 Alan Knight
7 Raymond Lister
9 John Bethell

The Lucys of Charlecote and their Library
by Henry Summerson
1-9 Joe Cocks Studio
10 Birmingham Reference Library (Sir Benjamin
Stone Collection)

Birds and Man on the County Antrim Coast
by Philip Watson
1 Aerofilms Ltd
2-12 G. Bond